ART

D0792833

Professional Careers Series

ART

BLYTHE CAMENSON

SECOND EDITION

New York Chicago San Francisco Lisbon London Madrid Mexico City
Milan New Delhi San Juan Seoul Singapore Sydney Toronto

Library of Congress Cataloging-in-Publication Data

Camenson, Blythe.
      Careers in art / Blythe Camenson.—2d ed.
          p.   cm.
      ISBN 0-07-146772-6 (alk. paper)
      1. Art—Vocational guidance—United States.   I. Title.

  N6505.C328   2006
  702'.373—dc22

                       2006006198

2 3 4 5 6 7 8 9 0   DSH/DSH   0 1 0 9 8

ISBN-13: 978-0-07-146772-8
ISBN-10: 0-07-146772-6

McGraw-Hill books are available at special quantity discounts to use as premiums and sales promotions, or for use in corporate training programs. For more information, please write to the Director of Special Sales, Professional Publishing, McGraw-Hill, Two Penn Plaza, New York, NY 10121-2298. Or contact your local bookstore.

This book is printed on acid-free paper.

CONTENTS

ACKNOWLEDGMENTS

I would like to thank the following professionals for providing insights into the world of art careers:

Jim Anderson, stained-glass artist
Edwin Ryan Bailey, artist and art instructor
Matthew Carone, art gallery owner
Aileen Chuk, associate registrar
Mindy Conley, art teacher
Karen Duvall, graphic designer
Elizabeth English, artist and illustrator; art gallery curator
Joan Gardner, chief conservator
Erica Hirshler, assistant curator
Deb Mason, potter
Peggy Peters, art teacher
Lynne Robins, art teacher
Rodney Stephens, framemaker

The editors wish to acknowledge the work of Josephine Scanlon in revising this book.

ART

C H A P T E R

1

INTRODUCTION TO THE FIELD

Successful artists might tell you that they never consciously chose a career in art—the profession chose them. Although skill in creating art is something that can be learned, refined, and honed, many people feel they came to their work with an inborn talent; it was just something they could always do.

Whether art is something you have always believed would be your calling, is an interest you have discovered, or a skill you actively sought out, numerous career choices await you. Reading this book will introduce you to the variety of settings in which you can work and the many job titles that fall under the heading of artist.

ART AS A COLLABORATIVE EFFORT

Many of us think of the creation of art as an individual effort, envisioning a solitary artist striving alone to turn out a finished work. While the actual work might be done individually, art as a whole does not stand alone. Rather, it functions within its own environment, in which each component is essential to the survival of the whole.

Human beings have been expressing themselves through art since the beginning of recorded history, laying the foundation for the environment in which art thrives. The need to create and share those creations has been an all-consuming force that even a millennium or two has not suppressed.

Even early cave paintings suggest a collaborative effort. Each clan artist must have had a teacher or mentor, and each clan undoubtedly had a historian, the storyteller who passed on significant events from one generation to another. Perhaps there was even a color and design expert to discuss pigment and the most aesthetic placement of drawings upon the walls.

The image of the starving artist painting alone in a garret belies the fact that collaboration continues, even today. Artists study, and are influenced by, those who came before them. Other individuals, working as art historians, delve deeply into the art of past cultures, and share that knowledge through their writings and teachings. Art educators contribute as well, teaching budding artists of any age the time-tested techniques and methods for creating a variety of art—from ceramics to computer graphics. Art critics add to the collaborative effort by helping to shape public tastes with their reviews. Museum curators and art gallery owners further the cause, choosing which art to display and which artists to promote.

The position you can fill in this environment is an individual choice, based on your interests, skills, and desires—the choices are varied. The degree of talent and skill you possess, the area that interests you, the amount of time you are willing to devote to study, the setting in which you prefer to work, and the kind of income you hope to earn will all influence the career path you choose.

Whichever road interests you most should be the one first explored. And if possible, you should begin that exploration at the beginning, with the question of education and training.

IS AN ART DEGREE NECESSARY?

Does the gifted prodigy necessarily need an art degree? Probably not. This rare individual has an inherent talent that allows him or her to create magnificent works of art without formal training. But even those who are extremely talented can still benefit from professional training. Learning about other artists can help shape our own creations, and the positive influence of a mentor can introduce the art student to new techniques and media.

Not all artists create art for art's sake—meaning that studio art is not the only path to follow. Many careers in art require a degree. Graphic artists, art educators, art curators, art historians, art restorers, art critics, art appraisers, and even art sellers must receive professional training and acquire sufficient experience to compete in the job market for these very popular fields.

In reality, most successful artists have pursued some form of higher education to hone their talent. Because educational options are as varied as the different careers in art, you must carefully consider which art program is right for you.

CHOOSING THE RIGHT ART PROGRAM

There are almost as many different names and focuses for art programs as there are job possibilities. Some of the most common designations are

- Applied arts
- Fine arts
- Cyberarts
- Computer arts
- Computer-aided design (CAD)
- Studio arts
- Art education
- Art history
- Museum studies
- Commercial arts
- Graphic arts
- Industrial arts
- Design
- Communication arts
- Visual arts

Art schools, institutes, colleges, and universities categorize their art programs in a variety of ways. In some institutions, the art department functions as part of the humanities department or college of liberal arts, while others have separate art schools. Still others feature art programs within the school of architecture, or offer a program that is combined with advertising, public relations, or other related disciplines.

Many university programs allow for a great deal of latitude in designing majors and courses of study. Many institutions offer interdisciplinary degrees, which can be beneficial to art majors who hope to teach. These programs can be particularly helpful with the decisions future art educators must make concerning their studies. Should they pursue a B.F.A. in their chosen subject area, and then work toward a teaching credential? Or should they study art education with a concentration in one of the subject areas?

There is no single correct answer. These decisions must be made individually, based on research into specific programs, personal long-term goals, and the availability of local programs or the ability to relocate if necessary.

SAMPLE ART PROGRAMS

Several art programs at various institutions are highlighted in this section to show how different schools focus their curricula. Ultimately, you must continue this research yourself: requesting catalogs, visiting campuses, and talking to other students and faculty members. An informed decision about your training program will only enhance your career opportunities.

University of Toledo: Art Education K–12

You may become an Ohio licensed art specialist for kindergarten through 12th grades upon completion of 128 to 135 hours of study, depending on your minor concentration.

The Art Education program of study is designed to develop your knowledge and skills as a student, teacher, and artist. Students must complete 39 hours of general education, ensuring a broad foundation in the liberal arts.

A critical element in the development of effective teaching skills is a strong professional background in the fundamentals of education. During this nine-hour component of the program, students will be introduced to the history, philosophy, and psychology of education, and will also have the opportunity to work in public schools to get a feel for the real world of teaching.

Coursework of nine hours in art education introduces the methods and techniques for teaching art making, art history, art criticism, and aesthetics. The 12-hour professional sequence in art education provides the final phase of teacher preparation. These courses include numerous field-based instructional opportunities, such as student teaching.

Central to the program of study is the development of your skills as an artist and craftsman. Specific content areas of study include 18 hours in two-dimensional studies such as drawing, painting, new media, design, and printmaking; nine hours in three-dimensional studies such as ceramics, metalsmithing, and sculpture; and nine hours in studio electives. Study of the history of art, which may include international travel, provides the final 12 hours of the core studies. Lastly, your program of study will be completed by selecting an additional nine hours of concentrated coursework in studio art, art history, or art education.

The Art Education Department offers a program in Early Childhood Art Education for both graduate and undergraduate students. The purpose of this program is to advance the skills and knowledge-base of an art educator to better address the developmental needs of the pre- and primary school child. This program promotes the use of art, aesthetics, art criticism, and art history to nurture the youngsters' physical, social, cognitive, and emotional development.

Rhode Island School of Design: Ceramics Department

The Rhode Island School of Design (RISD) offers 16 undergraduate majors from which to choose. As an example of what the school's programs offer, we will look at the Ceramics Department curriculum, which emphasizes strong technical development and a familiarity with ceramic science combined with expressive growth.

Students in the B.F.A. program become familiar with a variety of ceramic materials and processes, such as building by hand, molding, throwing, glazing, and firing. As students progress, they work in studios that focus on specific areas such as narrative sculpture and architectural ornamentation.

Students in their junior year work in the community, designing tableware for local restaurants and public tile installations. Seniors work in a tutorial setting and are expected to create a body of work that is unified in direction, significant in its degree of growth, innovative in its solutions, and personal in its expression.

The two-year M.F.A. program supports sculptural, decorative, and utilitarian approaches to ceramic materials and processes. Students participate in studio critiques and discussions, and attend a variety of seminars that investigate contemporary issues, the foundations of ceramics, and broader philosophical and critical theory. At the end of the program, students present a well-documented thesis for critical evaluation by the faculty.

Rice University, Houston: Department of Art History

Rice University is a small private school dedicated to the promotion of arts and letters, science, and engineering. As part of the university's School of Humanities, the Department of art history offers a wide range of courses in European, American, Asian, and Middle Eastern/Islamic art history, with additional strengths in architectural history and a program track in film and media studies. The major in art history is structured to expose students to the chronological, geographical, and methodological breadth of the field of scholarship.

Students with a single major in Art History must complete 36 hours (12 courses) in art history; those with double majors must complete 30 hours (ten courses). A total of six of the courses for double and single majors must be at the 300 level or above, and two of the courses must be in each of the following periods: Pre Modern, Early Modern, and Modern. Three of these six courses must be in American/European art history, distributed over the three periods, with one course in the Middle East/Islamic art history, which can be taken during any period. Of the 12/10 courses for single and double majors, at least two courses must be seminars.

It is strongly recommended that majors in Art History acquire a proficiency in at least one foreign language. In addition, Art History majors are encouraged to take advantage of the opportunities provided by museum internships, study-abroad programs, and travel fellowships.

University of Michigan, Ann Arbor: School of Art and Design

The School of Art and Design is committed to art practice that focuses on current issues, working with other schools and colleges of the university, as well as the local communities, to achieve its goals.

An example of the range of projects in which faculty and students participate is Detroit Connections, a collaborative program with various Detroit communities designed to use art to increase links with the city. Current projects include a science/art initiative for a Detroit elementary school, a public art project for reuse of an abandoned building, and a portable mural project.

Through the Distinguished Visitors Program, emerging and established artists and designers visit the school to interact with students and faculty. The school's exhibition program serves as the crucial juncture between studio work and public dialogue, providing a vital learning laboratory for students and an important educational resource for the university, the surrounding community, and beyond. The program includes three fully operational galleries that feature work by students, faculty, and staff, as well as that created by the broader national and international community of artists and designers.

Cross-disciplinary joint faculty appointments and connections with other units at the university enrich the educational environment. Faculty members conduct research and creative work that involves the community as well. International travel is a vital component of the Art and Design experience. Exchange agreements with partner institutions around the world provide international education experiences for both graduate and undergraduate students.

Minneapolis College of Art and Design

The design curriculum at the Minneapolis College of Art and Design teaches students how to identify and approach design problems, and how to find and execute creative and responsible solutions.

All design students begin with courses that examine the general principles of design and the techniques used by the designer. These courses draw from disciplines such as sociology, psychology, and anthropology to help students better understand cultural influences and their future clients.

In studio classes, students apply this knowledge and develop technical skills in hands-on projects. Through creative exercises they learn the techniques required for professional practice.

In the areas of graphic design, illustration, and advertising design, students generate ideas and imagery, use color, integrate images and text, and explore the dynamics of typography and page composition.

Furniture design students approach their studies from three key points of view: the creation of individual pieces from the artist's expression, the mastering of the ability to design for a specific purpose or patronage, and the skills of relating individualized designs to industrial processes.

Students with a graphic design, furniture design, or advertising specialization are required to take computer graphics courses. Computers are used in most design classes to produce work and are important tools for exploring and experimenting with alternative methods of solving typography and image problems. All design majors are required to take theory and methodology courses and to complete a senior project.

Montana State University, Bozeman: School of Art

The School of Art at Montana State University is a professional school within the College of Art and Architecture. The school offers courses leading to a B.A. degree with programs in ceramics, jewelry and metalsmithing, painting, drawing, graphic design, sculpture, art history, and art education. Montana State also offers an M.F.A. degree in ceramics, jewelry and metalsmithing, painting, drawing, and sculpture. The professional art program has a national reputation and offers the training and personal guidance necessary for a successful career in the visual arts. All programs are accredited by the National Association of Schools of Art and Design.

CAREER OPTIONS

The aim of this book is to help you narrow the wide range of choices and find the career path that best suits your education, interests, and skills.

The book explores five main art career options which are discussed throughout the following chapters under these primary categories:

- Graphic Arts
- Fine Arts
- Art Education
- Museum Studies
- Art Sales
- Art Appraisal

Although it is not exhaustive, this list of main tracks comprises hundreds of different job titles. As you read, research, and talk to other working artists and art educators, you may unearth several other possibilities that interest you.

Also, while reading many of the firsthand accounts included in the chapters ahead, you will often notice that artists don't limit themselves to one particular career track. Portrait artists also design T-shirts. Potters work in living history museums. Graphic artists do stints in art galleries. Sculptors work in advertising agencies.

Whichever track you ultimately choose, your decision to be flexible will ultimately broaden your employment options.

SAMPLE JOB LISTINGS

As a preview, take a look at the following samples of actual job listings. They offer an overview of the types of duties you would perform and the working conditions you can expect. They also specify the training you would need to qualify for each position.

Position: Art Director

A leader in the casual entertainment software industry is seeking a senior art director to join our team. The individual will be responsible for the art direction and design of classic game software titles. This hands-on creative position involves overseeing creative development, defining the look and feel of the product, and supervising artists. Primary production responsibilities include 2-D design and illustration; knowledge of 3-D helpful. Requires technical knowledge of art tools (Photoshop, DeBabelizer, FreeHand, After Effects) and development engines. Industrial design, graphic design, or related degree required. Minimum four to five years of professional design and supervisory experience. Familiarity with Internet applications a plus.

Position: Web Production Artist

A high-profile Internet commerce leader needs full-time web production artist to create banners, scan and touch up artwork, create original elements for the existing site, and contribute to the design of our new site slated for next year. We're looking for someone who is creative and highly organized, has a great sense of humor, and understands the power of good design. We need someone with strong Photoshop, ImageReady, DeBabelizer, and scanning skills, as well as a good understanding of image compression and web palette issues. (Flash and HTML skills are a plus.) Must be Windows and Mac literate.

Position: Senior Designer for Travel Magazine

A national consumer magazine has a position for a full-time graphic designer. Applicants must have magazine experience and an interest in travel. This is a full-time salaried position.

Position: Graphic Designer

Hip interactive point-of-purchase merchandising company seeks flexible graphic designer to help bring hot new projects to life. Candidates must be familiar with the latest graphic design and DTP tools (Photoshop, Illustrator, PageMaker, Quark XPress, etc.), but, ideally, also be able to do some work with traditional materials. If you're ready to exercise creative license and can thrive in a dynamic environment, send your resume to us.

Position: Graphic Artist

With over 600 retail superstores and record-breaking sales of more than $6.7 billion, our growth continues. Join us now in our fast-paced advertising department. Requires proficiency in Quark XPress with a minimum of five years' experience. Knowledge of retail advertising for production of catalogs, direct mail, and newspapers a plus.

Position: Illustrator

A well-established greeting card company seeks talented illustrator and cartoonist. Prior related experience preferred. B.F.A. or M.F.A. preferred but successful portfolio may substitute for formal degree. Send cover letter, resume, and slides.

Position: Art Curator

Opening for a curator of visual resources; reports to assistant director, collection development, and curatorial projects. Develops coherent plan for managing collection of 1.75 million study photographs of art and architecture. Implements organizational, cataloguing, and preservation work plans to enhance scholarly understanding and accessibility. Participates in museum's overall collection development programs, acts as subject bibliographer, and recommends acquisitions of special collections and visual resources materials. Conducts scholarly research, provides advanced reference, and participates in activities including exhibitions, lectures, and publications. Requires Ph.D. in art history or related humanities discipline, or equivalent combination of training and experience; comprehensive knowledge of the history of art with two or more specialized research fields within the broad areas of Mediterranean archaeology and European art from the Middle Ages to the 19th century; fluency in relevant languages plus reading ability in two other western European languages.

Position: Exhibits Registrar

Registrar is responsible for creating, organizing, and maintaining orderly forms, legal documents, files, and retrieval systems. Organizes, documents, and coordinates all aspects of borrowing and lending objects, including handling, packing, and shipping of objects. Will supervise implementation of a collections management database and maintain the database and records associated with the art collection. Required qualifications: bachelor's degree or equivalent; minimum two years' experience in museum registration, fine arts shipping, or related experience; knowledge of conservation and storage practices, legal matters related to the collection, copyright laws and policies governing rights and reproductions, insurance requirements for the collections, and packing techniques and transportation methods; demonstrated ability to plan and implement multiple projects and work independently; flexibility in originating sound solutions; ability to work in an organized manner; ability to travel two to three weeks at a time.

Position: Exhibits Technician

One of the nation's most prominent and historic sites has an excellent opportunity for a hands-on individual with experience in building and maintaining exhibits and handling artifacts. Requires minimum two years' relevant experience and proficiency in carpentry, fabrication, and basic art skills. An interest in U.S. military history is a plus. We offer competitive salary and benefits.

Position: Art Instructor

Full-time art instructor to instruct freshman and sophomore art theory and studio courses within a one-person department. Minimum requirements are a master's degree in education with 24-hours' concentration in art or an M.F.A. Preference for community college experience. Eligible for state postsecondary licensure. Salary commensurate with experience.

Position: Art Educator

Fixed-term, one-year position. Ph.D. in art education preferred. Teach undergraduate art education and participate in the elementary program. Advising, relevant research, creative work, and service to community expected. The Art Department employs ten faculty members and offers over 240 majors for B.A., B.S., B.F.A., M.A., and M.S. degrees. NASAD accredited. Excellent resources, library, gallery, visiting artist program.

Position: Art Instructor, Sculpture/Ceramics

College seeks applications for a two-year non-tenure-track term position at the assistant professor level. Teaching responsibilities will include two offerings each of beginning to intermediate sculpture, beginning to intermediate ceramics, and a 2-D/3-D design course. M.F.A. in sculpture (preferred) or ceramics and a minimum of two years of college-level teaching experience required. Salary competitive and consistent with level of experience. Candidates are expected to have high aptitude and interest in undergraduate teaching, a commitment to the liberal arts, and a desire to involve undergraduates in creative work both inside and outside the classroom. Send letter of application, curriculum vitae, slide portfolio of recent work, undergraduate and graduate transcripts (unofficial acceptable), a detailed statement of teaching philosophy and goals, and three letters of recommendation.

YOUR JOB SEARCH

The sample job listings give you an idea of what's out there. When you're ready to start your job search, you can use conventional methods like newspaper ads, word of mouth, the Internet, job and recruitment fairs, direct calls, and blind resume submissions. But each job discussed in this book also has its own avenues to pursue. The following chapters will lead you to those avenues and get you started in the right direction.

GRAPHIC ARTS

The term "visual arts" covers the fields of graphic arts and illustration as well as studio or fine arts. This chapter focuses on careers in graphic arts; the next chapter discusses studio or fine arts.

Graphic artists (also known as commercial artists) and illustrators offer their artistic skills and vision to commercial clients such as major corporations, retail stores, and advertising, design, or publishing firms. Artists working in this area generally have greater job security than the studio or fine artist, although a regular paycheck often means sacrificing some of the artistic freedom that studio artists enjoy.

Graphic artists, whether freelancers or employed by a firm, use a variety of print, electronic, and film media to create art that meets a client's needs. Increasingly, they use computers instead of such traditional tools as pens, pencils, scissors, and color strips to produce their work. Computers enable them to lay out and test various designs, formats, and colors before printing a final design.

WHAT GRAPHIC ARTISTS DO

Graphic artists perform different jobs depending on their areas of expertise and the needs of their employers. Some work for only one employer, while others work as freelancers and are employed by a variety of clients.

Graphic Designers

Graphic designers, who usually design on a two-dimensional level, may create packaging and promotional displays for a new product, the visual design for an annual report and other corporate literature, or a distinctive logo for a product or business. They also help with the layout and design of magazines, newspapers, journals, and other publications, and create graphics for television. An increasing number of graphic designers are developing material for Internet web pages, computer interfaces, and multimedia projects. Graphic designers also produce the credits that appear before and after television programs and movies.

Illustrators

Illustrators paint or draw pictures for films; books, magazines, and other publications; and paper products such as greeting cards, calendars, wrapping paper, and stationery. Many create a variety of illustrations, while others specialize in a particular style.

Medical and Scientific Illustrators

Medical and scientific illustrators combine artistic skills with a knowledge of the biological sciences. Medical illustrators draw human anatomy and surgical procedures, while scientific illustrators sketch animals and plants. These illustrations are used in medical and scientific publications, and in audiovisual presentations for teaching purposes. Medical illustrators also work for physicians and for lawyers, producing exhibits for court cases.

Fashion Artists

Fashion artists draw women's, men's, and children's clothing and accessories for newspapers, magazines, and other media.

Storyboard Illustrators

Storyboard illustrators draw storyboards for TV commercials. Storyboards present TV commercials in a series of scenes similar to a comic strip, so an advertising agency and client (the company doing the advertising) can evaluate proposed commercials. Storyboards may also serve as guides regarding the placement of actors and cameras, as well as other important details necessary to the production of commercials.

Cartoonists

Cartoonists draw political, advertising, social, and sports cartoons. Some collaborate with writers, but most cartoonists have humorous, critical, or dramatic talents in addition to their drawing skills.

Animators

Animators work in the motion picture and television industries. They draw by hand and use computers to create the large series of pictures that, when transferred to film or tape, form the animated cartoons seen in movies and on TV.

Art Directors

Art directors, also called visual journalists, review the text of periodicals, newspapers, and other printed media, and decide how to visually present the information in an eye-catching yet organized manner. They make decisions about which photographs or artwork to use and generally oversee production of the printed material.

WORKING LIFESTYLES

Graphic artists work in art and design studios located in office buildings or in their own homes. They are employed by publishing companies and art and design studios, and generally work a standard forty-hour week. During busy periods, they may work overtime to meet deadlines.

Self-employed graphic artists can set their own hours but may spend much time and effort selling their services to potential customers or clients and establishing a reputation. Many graphic artists work part-time as freelancers while continuing in a full-time job until they become established.

Others have enough talent, perseverance, and confidence in their abilities to start freelancing full-time immediately after they graduate from art school. Many take on freelance projects while still enrolled in school in order to gain experience and acquire a portfolio of published work.

The successful freelance artist develops a set of clients who regularly contract for work. Some freelancers are widely recognized for their skill in specialties such as children's book illustration, magazine illustration, or design. These artists can earn high incomes and can pick and choose the type of work they do.

Most freelance careers, however, take time to build. While making contacts and developing skills, many find work in various organizations. Still other commercial artists prefer full-time employment over freelancing.

EMPLOYMENT SETTINGS

The following are some of the various settings in which full-time graphic artists can find work.

Advertising Agencies and Design Firms

Graphic artists hired by advertising agencies or design studios often start with relatively routine work. During this time, many enterprising graphic artists also practice their skills on the side. Jobs can cover anything from direct-mail pieces to catalog work, posters, and even aspects of the television and motion picture industries.

Publishing Companies

Magazine, newspaper, and book publishers require the expertise of commercial artists for a wide range of jobs. These include cover design, advertising layout, typesetting, and graphics.

Department Stores

Department stores, especially the larger chains, routinely produce catalogs, direct-mail pieces, fliers, posters, and a variety of other advertising and promotional material. While small stores might send the work out to freelancers, large department stores often have fully staffed departments to handle the workload.

Television and Motion Picture Industries

The worlds of television and film are wide open territory for graphic artists. Organizations such as Disney, for example, actively recruit new graduates right out of art schools and offer very attractive salaries. Opportunities are especially strong for those with established skills in computer graphics.

Other Businesses and Government Agencies

Other employment settings for graphic artists include manufacturing firms and the various agencies with local, state, and federal governments.

THE QUALIFICATIONS YOU'LL NEED

Now that you know some of the varied and interesting places that graphic artists might find work, it's time to consider the qualifications that you will need in order to establish a career in this interesting field.

Graphic Arts

A successful graphic artist needs to show demonstrated ability and appropriate training or other qualifications. Most art and design directors, as well as other employers, will look to the artist's portfolio for evidence of talent and skill. The portfolio is a valuable tool for the artist, serving as a resume that helps an employer or client decide whether to hire an artist for a particular job.

The portfolio is a collection of the artist's best work, whether handmade, computer generated, or print. In theory, a person with a good portfolio but no training or experience could succeed in graphic arts. In reality, however, assembling an impressive portfolio requires skills generally developed in a postsecondary art or design school program, such as a bachelor's degree program in fine arts, graphic design, or visual communications.

Internships also provide excellent opportunities for artists and designers to develop and enhance their portfolios. Most programs in art and design also provide training in computer design techniques. This training is becoming increasingly important as a qualification for many jobs in commercial art.

Medical Illustration

Those who hope to work in medical illustration need very specific training and skills. In addition to artistic ability, medical illustrators must have detailed knowledge of living organisms, surgical and medical procedures, and human and sometimes animal anatomy. A four-year bachelor's degree combining art and premedical courses is usually required, followed by a master's degree in medical illustration, a degree offered by only a small number of accredited schools.

THE JOB HUNT

As in most any professional career, contacts and having a foot in the door at the type of organization where you'd like to work are valuable assets. Internships can be the pathway to both.

The best strategy for finding a job is to plan ahead. During your undergraduate or graduate studies, arrange for as many internships as you can squeeze in, either full-time during the summers or part-time during semesters.

An internship at an advertising agency, PR firm, or TV studio will give you a broad overview of that field. It will also help you build a successful portfolio. If an internship gives you a foot in the door, a professional and creative portfolio can open that door all the way. In addition, find yourself a mentor, someone who can critique your portfolio and advise you on how best to proceed.

A good resource for those seeking internships is *Peterson's Internships*, an annual publication that provides information on how to choose and apply for internships in a wide range of areas. The book is listed in Appendix D.

GETTING AHEAD

In general, illustrators advance as their work circulates and as they establish a reputation for a particular style. The best illustrators continue to try new ideas, and their work constantly evolves over time.

Graphic artists within firms may advance to assistant art director, art director, design director, and in some companies, creative director of an art or design department. Some may gain enough skill to succeed as freelancers, or they may prefer to specialize in a particular area. Others decide to open their own businesses.

INCOME

According to the most recent available data from the U.S. Bureau of Labor Statistics, median annual earnings for graphic designers were $36,680 in 2002. The middle 50 percent earned between $28,140 and $48,820. The lowest 10 percent earned less than $21,860, while the highest 10 percent earned more than $64,160. Median annual earnings in the industries employing the largest numbers of graphic designers were as follows:

Advertising and related services	$39,510
Specialized design services	$38,710
Printing and related support activities	$31,800
Newspaper, periodical, book, and directory publishers	$31,670

Well-established freelancers may earn much more than salaried artists. Like other independent workers, however, self-employed artists must provide their own health insurance benefits.

CAREER OUTLOOK

Employment of designers overall is expected to increase about 20 percent through 2012, with most new jobs occurring in graphic design. Demand for graphic designers should increase because of the rapidly expanding market for web-based information and expansion of the video entertainment market, including television, movies, video, and made-for-Internet outlets.

Those hoping to enter this field should expect to face keen competition for available positions since many talented individuals are attracted to careers as designers. Those with little or no formal education in design, as well as those who lack creativity and perseverance, will find it very difficult to establish and maintain a career in the occupation.

Graphic designers held 212,000 jobs in 2002, and worked primarily in specialized design services; newspaper, periodical, book, and directory publishers; and advertising and related services. A large proportion of designers were self-employed and did freelance work—full-time or part-time—in addition to holding a salaried job in design or another occupation.

INTERVIEW

Elizabeth English, Artist/Illustrator

Elizabeth English works as an artist/illustrator for a literary and film production company in Boulder, Colorado. She has worked as an artist for over 25 years. Elizabeth earned her B.F.A. at C. W. Post College in Greenvale, Long Island, New York in 1976. She has also done substantial graduate work at a variety of institutions, including Hunter College, the State University of New York in Farmingdale, the University of Colorado in Boulder, and the Pratt Institute in Brooklyn.

Elizabeth provides some valuable insights into getting started as an artist and what the work really involves. As you'll see, she is like many artists who have worked in a variety of settings. You can read her firsthand account of working as a curator for an art gallery in Chapter 6. Here she talks about her career as a freelance artist.

Like many artists, Elizabeth has always known that she would make her living through creativity. As she says, "I didn't choose the field of art, it chose me! I've been doing artwork since I could hold a crayon. I never thought of doing anything else, along with the writing I also do."

Elizabeth began her training by majoring in art in high school. She received a full scholarship to attend college, where she continued her art studies because she enjoyed the satisfaction she received from expressing herself creatively. In addition to her formal education, Elizabeth worked as a curator in an art gallery, pored over countless art books, and traveled the world observing as much art as possible.

Her best training, however, came from continuing to practice her art, whether it involved drawing and painting, pottery, sculpture, cartooning, stained glass, or weaving. Elizabeth also went on archeological expeditions and documented prehistoric rock art and ethnic arts and crafts around the world.

She got her first job in the art field after putting on an art show during her senior year in high school. All of her works sold, and one of the buyers, who owned an advertising agency, offered her a job as the agency artist. Her responsibilities included creating logos, label designs, and ads.

Elizabeth later worked for a newspaper, where she created artwork for advertisements, and designed characters and print campaigns. In addition, the paper published several of her political and topical cartoons.

Today, Elizabeth works as a freelance artist, primarily involved in animation for feature films. She designs the characters, backgrounds, costumes, interiors, and logos for animated features, sometimes writing screenplays for the films and lyrics for the songs.

Elizabeth also works as a fine artist on commission for private clients, with hundreds of her artworks now privately owned. In this capacity, she creates large-scale sculptures in metal, as well as paintings, tapestries, stained glass, pottery, and weavings. Occasionally, she simply designs the art, and other artists create it under her supervision.

In addition to all this, Elizabeth works as a consultant for individuals and corporations. She is paid to travel within the world of museums, galleries, and artists' studios to purchase paintings for her clients. Elizabeth is responsible for having the works matted and framed, and installed in private homes, hotels, restaurants, offices, and even palaces in Saudi Arabia.

Aside from her work as an artist, Elizabeth has also written several children's books. Not surprisingly, she has created the illustrations for the books herself. She has also written a series of contemporary cartoons and created cover art specifically for *The New Yorker* magazine. Meanwhile, Elizabeth is writing and illustrating an encyclopedia of the art, lore, and mythology of mermaids. This involves a good deal of travel and research in addition to the artwork.

As mentioned earlier, another of Elizabeth's interests is filmmaking, and in addition to her endeavors in animation she has produced several documentary films for which she served as art director and production designer. She also plans to produce music videos in the future.

To round out her portfolio, Elizabeth has found additional work as an interior designer, set designer, costume designer, and lighting designer.

Given her varied interests, it's not easy to imagine what a typical day might be like for Elizabeth. "I choose to do whatever project most interests me on any particular day," she says. "Or, if I have a deadline, I focus on that project first."

Much of Elizabeth's time is spent attracting clients, which she accomplishes by sending query letters and samples of her work and credits.

She also spends a lot of time designing artwork and preparing sketches for her clients' approval.

When asked what she likes most about working as an artist, Elizabeth responds, "My job is fascinating, satisfying, and creative, and I feel it helps others to see the world in a different way and to appreciate both the beauties of nature and their fellow human beings in a new light.

"The day goes by so quickly when I am being an artist and either drawing, designing, painting, or whatever, that sometimes I work into the night without realizing that I forgot dinner.

"I can work in the middle of the night, work 18 hours without stopping, take days off if I feel like it. I can work wearing my robe and nightgown all day, or I can go for a hike with my dog and take my drawing or painting supplies and create art out in nature, observing the world."

Another benefit is the opportunity to travel. Elizabeth occasionally travels to Europe or Asia to paint and sketch for a few weeks. She has visited Provence, Tuscany, Greece, and Japan. She also still enjoys documenting prehistoric rock art at archeological sites such as those in the American southwest and Patagonia.

Elizabeth's career affords her another advantage that not everyone can claim. She says, "Another good thing about working as an artist is that most clients know very little about the arts, and you are left to do your work without interference or suggestions from the boss! I also like working freelance, because I can set my own hours and working situation. The pay is usually very good, and I have made a fine living as an artist for many years. Plus, I have the pleasure of seeing my work in people's homes and in offices, hotels, and other settings."

Aside from all these benefits, Elizabeth is also honest about the downside of her career. She explains, "In illustration, many clients want something specific and you must work to satisfy their needs rather than being wholly creative. Also, there is not as much money in illustration as in fine arts. In fine arts, however, it is very difficult to get your work sold, unless you have steady clientele or a big name."

Salaries in the art world can vary considerably. In Elizabeth's case, she says, "I have not worked for a salary for so many years. Freelance is my preference. I have been paid $25,000 for one sculpture, $10,000 for a painting, $10,000 for stained glass, $5,000 for a weaving."

Elizabeth points out that the pay is lower in illustration and cartooning, but varies depending on the employer. A small local newspaper might pay only $25 for a published cartoon or illustration, while a major magazine would pay between $500 and $1,000. A magazine cover could earn thousands of dollars. Music videos pay upwards of $50,000 for artwork. Illustrations for children's books might start at around $1,000, but could earn $10,000 or more if the book is an award-winning bestseller.

Given the extent of her creative endeavors, it is not surprising that Elizabeth has some sound advice for aspiring artists.

"Be creative always. Think like an artist. Live as an artist. Persevere and never give up. Practice your art. Diversify! Be a painter, a sculptor. Do drawings using everything from crayons to charcoal to pencil to pen to Japanese brushwork. Study the arts and methods of artists of other cultures and other times. Learn stained glass, pottery, and other crafts.

"Go to museums, art shows, and gallery openings. Read everything you can on the arts: books and magazines. Read the book *The Artist's Way* by Julia Cameron and follow her advice. Attend a good art school. Make up a great—not just good but great—portfolio of your best diversified artwork."

To sum up her own perspective on her career, Elizabeth says, "I love having the opportunity to be creative and to express myself. Being an artist allows me to do that and make a living at the same time."

INTERVIEW

Karen Duvall, Graphic Designer

Karen Duvall is a graphic designer with Publication Design, Inc. in Denver, Colorado, a full-service agency specializing in magazine publications. She has worked in the field since 1978. Karen has an associate's degree in advertising design from the Colorado Institute of Art in Denver.

"I started drawing at a very early age," Karen says, "since before I could even walk (according to my mother). I've known all my life that I would be an artist."

The advertising design program that Karen attended at the Colorado Institute of Art was an intense year-round program with six-hour days of instructions each week for two years. The Institute focuses exclusively on graphic design, so Karen received a solid foundation for her work as a result of the program.

Her first job after art school was working as a teacher's aide to an art teacher at an elementary school. She next worked as the graphics manager for a gift manufacturer, but was laid off when the company decided that creating packaging for their products was too expensive.

Suddenly without a job, Karen contacted everyone she knew in the business, as well as some ad agencies. She also posted her resume online and answered job ads posted on various career web sites. Within a week she was in contact with a designer she had worked with previously, who was the creative director for Publication Design, Inc., her current employer. The designer asked Karen to substitute for him for five days while he was away from the office, and that opportunity turned into a full-time offer when another designer resigned. Karen says, "The moral of this story is to always keep track of the contacts you make in your field; you never know when you might need them."

When asked what her job is like, Karen refers to one of her completed projects as the best way to describe what she does. A client needed a promotional piece that could be mailed to prospective customers, and wanted something unique. Since the budget was large, Karen was free to experiment with different ideas. She created a pop-up card that was a complicated three-dimensional design. The piece was colorful and contained a direct message that clearly expressed the client's point.

While managing this project, Karen was involved in many client meetings and created several proofs for the client's approval. She also dealt directly with the printer who manufactured the card and was responsible for checking proofs throughout the process. The client was very pleased with the finished product, which the printer entered in the annual National Packaging Awards competition.

Although most of Karen's projects are interesting to her, not all are as involved as the one she described. She also creates brochures and advertisements for newspapers and magazines. The company designs logos and corporate communication material, book covers, consumer product labels, and training materials. As Karen says, "You name it, we'll design it!"

Karen does all of her design and illustration work on a Macintosh computer, using such programs as Photoshop, Illustrator, Quark XPress, and Painter. All of the company's artists have Wacom tablets with a laser stylus for easy drawing and painting on the computer. Since the digital art files created can become quite large, their hard drives allow for several gigabytes of storage, and the company has a large archive system and several network servers.

Karen describes the office atmosphere as generally relaxed, although it can become tense when deadlines approach or there are equipment failures. The designers work a standard 40-hour week, with occasional overtime.

Since all the artists have home computers, the company allows them to take work home now and then and pays them overtime for the extra effort.

When asked about the best part of her job, Karen says, "I'm lucky to have a position that's extremely creative, and because of my experience, my employer gives me free rein on the projects I undertake. I've been a designer long enough that I'm completely trusted in my design directions and the methods I use to develop my projects."

What Karen dislikes about her job is the need to repeat work due to a client's indecision. She explains, "What I like least are the clients who can't make up their minds and constantly make changes, so it's like doing a project completely over, again and again and again. I consider it a waste of valuable time. But at least we bill by the hour."

Karen says that her salary falls between $35,000 and $40,000 per year, but with overtime she often exceeds the average. She advises that graphic design salaries are typically unstructured, and the pay rate is up to the employer. The local cost of living is also a factor, as is the experience an artist brings to the job. The industry is highly competitive, and there is a high demand for talented graphic artists.

"A good graphic artist is someone who can do more than draw pretty pictures," Karen says. "They must also be knowledgeable in client and vendor relations, have technical experience in the tools of the trade, be well-versed in all areas of prepress production, have an ability to conceptualize a solution to a visual communications problem, and have an optimistic attitude."

As in other areas of art, freelancers in graphic design can make far more money than the average salary. While a freelancer might earn as much as $100 per hour, freelance jobs are unpredictable and may not be able to provide you with a living wage. However, Karen suggests that freelancing is a good way to supplement your regular income. She says, "Though I limit the number of freelance jobs I undertake (I can afford to be picky), it allows me great versatility and some pretty snappy samples for my portfolio."

Based on her own experience, Karen advises that a successful graphic artist is one who pays his or her dues while moving up in the ranks. The graphic arts field is extremely broad and far more versatile than most people realize, and Karen has learned that changing jobs, broadening your range of skills, and experimenting with the different aspects of the industry can create much greater opportunities for any developing career.

"Creative talent is your foundation for success, but you'll need far more than that to be truly successful," Karen says. "A good art school is an adequate start, but that education won't take you very far. Most schools are inept at providing you with the skills and expertise essential to making it in a real graphics job. They focus on the fun stuff, the creative puffery that does more for the ego than anything else, and end up inflating a fledgling artist's expectations of a successful graphics career. I personally have trained many recent graduates, most of whom had no clue how to function as a productive artist in the working world. So a school can only give you the bare basics; the rest is up to you."

Karen suggests that anyone who is seriously interested in pursuing a career in graphic arts should develop their observation skills. Even while you're attending art school, you should still concentrate on your own self-education by meeting professionals in your chosen field and asking lots of questions. Request a tour of a print shop and have someone take you from prepress to stripping to platemaking, and then to the actual presses. Ask questions such as: What are the biggest problems you encounter when working with graphic designers? What do you suggest to help prevent me from making the same mistakes? Also, visit service bureaus and observe what actually goes into running electronic files to film. See how match prints are made, learn what an Iris is, and understand exactly how the four-color process works to create a full-color image. Do you know what a color build is? What's spot color? What's the difference between a sheetfed press and a web press, and how does the quality differ? What's digital printing, and is it better than offset? What line screen is best for printing your particular project? How is silk-screen printing done, and why are the process and inks used different from other methods of printing? What's flexography? What's thermography? What's the difference between aqueous coating and UV? This is all very basic stuff, all elements that can have a dramatic effect on your design, and very little of it will ever be covered in art school.

"Graphic design goes far beyond the first step of creating something that looks nice," Karen says. "You must know and understand the end results of a printed piece of artwork before you can effectively initiate the creation of one."

3

FINE ARTS

You have completed an accredited art degree program, and have practiced and honed your skills through your own perseverance. You have long held the goal of supporting yourself as an artist or craftsperson, perhaps even opening your own studio. Whether your passion and talent lie in pottery or painting, sewing or stained glass, you believe that you can make a name for yourself and work full-time in your chosen area.

Even with the best preparation and belief in your ability and potential, it is important to keep in mind that few studio artists can move immediately into a career that provides adequate financial support right from the outset. It takes time to build a reputation and establish a clientele. During those early "lean years," many artists pursue additional avenues that can assure them of a regular paycheck.

Although some artists might moonlight in a number of different occupations—anything from food service to secretarial work—the vast majority choose to stay in related fields. Those with a teaching certificate might teach art in elementary or secondary schools, while those with a master's or doctoral degree might teach in colleges or universities.

Some fine artists work in arts administration in city, state, or federal arts programs. Others may work as art critics, art consultants, or as directors or representatives in fine art galleries, or they may be employed as private art instructors, or curators setting up art exhibits in museums. You will find talented artists working in a variety of settings, many of which are covered in this and other chapters of this book.

GOALS

The main goal of the serious studio artist is to create a work of art that combines self-expression with the need to make a living. It can be done.

Fine arts (also known as studio arts) and graphic arts make up the two categories that fall under the umbrella of the visual arts. Their difference depends not so much on the medium as on the artist's purpose in creating a work of art. Graphic artists, many of whom own their own studios, put their artistic skills and vision at the service of commercial clients, such as major corporations, retail stores, and advertising, design, or publishing firms. Studio artists, on the other hand, often create art to satisfy their own need for self-expression; they may display their work in museums, corporate collections, art galleries, and private homes. Some of their work may be done upon their clients' request, but this doesn't happen as frequently as in the case of graphic artists.

Fine artists usually work independently, choosing whatever subject matter and medium suits them. Usually, they specialize in one or two (or more) forms of art.

THE DISCIPLINES

Studio artists use an almost limitless variety of methods and materials to communicate ideas, thoughts, and feelings. They employ oils, watercolors, acrylics, pastels, magic markers, pencils, pen and ink, silk screen, plaster, clay, or any of a number of other media, including computers, to create realistic and abstract works or images of objects, people, nature, topography, or events. The following examples describe just a few of the many fine arts disciplines.

Painters

These artists generally work with two-dimensional art forms. Using techniques of shading, perspective, and color-mixing, painters produce works that depict realistic scenes or that may evoke different moods and emotions, depending on the artist's goals.

Sculptors

These three-dimensional artists either mold and join materials such as clay, glass, wire, plastic, or metal, or cut and carve forms from a block of plaster, wood, or stone. Some sculptors combine various materials such as concrete, metal, wood, plastic, and paper.

Potters

Working with a variety of clay materials—from low-fire clays to high-fire stoneware or porcelain—potters either handcraft their artwork or create different forms using a potter's wheel. They follow existing glaze recipes or experiment with different chemicals to formulate their own finishes.

Printmakers

Printmakers create printed images from designs cut into wood, stone, or metal, or from computer-driven data. The designs may be engraved as in the case of woodblocking, etched as in the manner of etchings, or derived from computers in the form of ink-jet or laser prints.

Stained-Glass Artists

Working with glass, paints, leading, wood, and other materials, these artists create functional as well as decorative artwork such as windows, skylights, or doors.

Photographers

Photographers utilize their cameras, lenses, film, and darkroom chemicals the way painters use paint and canvas. They capture realistic scenes of people, places, and events, or through the use of various techniques (both natural and contrived) they create photographs that elicit a variety of moods and emotions.

GETTING AHEAD

Fine artists advance as their work circulates and as they establish a reputation for having a particular style. The best artists continue to experiment with new ideas, and their work constantly evolves over time.

WORKING LIFESTYLES

Artists generally work in art and design studios located in commercial buildings or in their own home studios. Some artists prefer to work alone, while others like working with fellow artists. For the latter group, sharing space with other artists is often a viable alternative to the lone studio—both for stimulation and to reduce costs. The trend in many large cities (and even in less populated areas) is toward shared space in cooperatively owned studios, or rented space in converted warehouses or storefronts.

While artists generally require well-lighted and ventilated surroundings, some art forms in particular demand a safer and healthier work environment given the odors and dust from glues, paint, ink, clay, or other materials.

INTERVIEW

Edwin Ryan Bailey, Studio Artist

Edwin Ryan Bailey is a self-employed artist in Winter Haven, Florida and has been a professional artist since 1979. Ryan, as he is called, earned his B.F.A. degree in illustration and design from Auburn University in Alabama in 1985 and his M.F.A. in studio art from Florida State University in Tallahassee in 1991.

Like many artists, Ryan began drawing as a toddler, and says that by second grade he was telling people he wanted to be an artist when he grew up. He feels fortunate that his parents and teachers recognized and encouraged his talent. Although there were few professional artists in the rural Alabama area where Ryan grew up, he continued to pursue his interests.

In 1979, when he was a high-school junior, Ryan took out a loan and rented a building in his hometown of Lineville, Alabama. He opened Ryan's Art Studio, his first professional space, where he sold painting supplies and taught private lessons. He also did commissioned work, including paintings, portraits, and most of the town's signs.

While he owned the studio, Ryan taught himself to airbrush and began printing shirts, which he sold at craft fairs during summers and on weekends. He says, "I really had no idea what an artist did or what types of jobs were out there. I simply created my own niche." Ryan sold the business when he moved away to college.

Although he had practiced art since childhood, Ryan's real education began in college. He says, "As a child I had taken private lessons, but the real eye-opener came when I entered college at Auburn University. Many of my classmates had studied commercial art in high school, whereas I didn't even know what a T-square was. There were two options, fine arts or illustration/design. I took as many classes as I could in both fields.

"Like most things worth doing, it is a continual process of upgrading oneself. I constantly study and try to learn new techniques and improve upon old ones. It requires continual practice."

To pay his way through college, Ryan returned to airbrushing T-shirts. He spent the summer at the beach where he worked at a T-shirt shop, and did as well there financially as some of the graduates in his field did working year-round at entry-level illustration jobs. He continued the T-shirt work for many years, supplementing his earnings from commissioned illustrations and paintings.

During this period, Ryan heard of an opening for an adjunct instructor for the airbrush class in the fine arts department at Gulf Coast Community College. With his B.F.A., experience in airbrushing techniques, and an interest in teaching, Ryan knew that this position was an excellent opportunity. He began working at the college in 1988, and continued his own education while teaching others. He commuted two hours to Florida State University in Tallahassee to work toward his M.F.A., which then qualified him to teach additional art courses.

Although he enjoys teaching, Ryan admits that it can present an obstacle for a freelance artist. He began teaching to fill in the off season at the beach, but ultimately the teaching became much more important to him. "Soon I was falling into the art teacher trap," Ryan explains, "where teaching takes away from studio time and you soon find you're not making art. Time for the studio has to be set aside."

Ryan tries to keep to a regular work schedule. Although his studio is in his home, he disciplines himself to "go to work" every day. As he describes his day, "I get up every morning just like someone leaving to go to work, shower, get dressed, and go to the 'studio.' You have to forget the old cliché about 'the artist's mood'; there's no such thing. It's a response to habit. You must develop the habit of creativity and just do it."

Flexibility is important, however, since an artist never knows when an opportunity for new work might occur. As an example, Ryan describes a telephone call he received while painting in his studio. A federal trial was being moved from Atlanta to Panama City, where Ryan lived, and the television news station needed a courtroom artist to cover the proceedings. The local art center where Ryan volunteers offered his name, which indicates how community involvement can also be beneficial to a working artist.

Although he had never been in a courtroom, Ryan did have experience with figure drawing and portrait painting, so he offered to send the station a portfolio of his work. However, since the trial was beginning in four days, the station asked him to fax some samples immediately so they could make a decision. Ryan convinced them to wait until the following day, and then conducted his own research into illustration books and articles on courtroom artists. He spent the evening watching Court TV, sketching directly from the television screen. The next day he faxed the work and was in court sketching on Monday.

When asked to describe how his career differs from that of a commercial artist, Ryan points out that while every art career has stressful aspects, commercial artists face more deadlines than studio artists do. As he says, "I remember responding to ads for illustration jobs and asking when would be a good time to come by. The answer was usually the same. 'It doesn't matter. Any time is a good time. We're here from 9 A.M. until 3 A.M. or until the job is done.'

"They were serious. Go to any college campus and drive by the art building any time day or night. The lights are always on with students meeting deadlines. The same goes for any design firm. They're always there."

What Ryan likes most about his job is that it gives him the opportunity to use his talent every day. He is regularly able to create art and to select which projects he wants to work on. He can set his own hours and dress casually. Perhaps the greatest satisfaction comes from watching a work of art go from conception to completion.

The thing that Ryan likes least is that he never seems to have a day off. As he says, "Any day could be a day in the studio—and since it's at home, it's as though I never leave work."

Another drawback is that arts and crafts shows are held on weekends, so Ryan's personal time is often tied up. When he was a T-shirt artist, he worked seven days a week in the summer, and for 17 years he worked on Memorial Day, Fourth of July, and Labor Day. As Ryan says, "Everyone else's holidays are your workdays."

Ryan finds that the most difficult aspect of working as a professional artist is earning respect. He has found that although people respect an artist's talent, they often don't see him as someone who really works, regardless of his earning potential. He also feels that people who work at home receive less respect as workers than those who go to an office every day. As he says, "No one would impose upon someone leaving to go to a building from nine to five like they would upon someone who is, presumably, hanging around the house all day."

Ryan advises anyone who wants to work as a professional artist to have several portfolios. He maintains one portfolio of his fine art for galleries, one of his courtroom sketches for the media, and another one of illustrations and computer art for businesses and publishers. When he was designing T-shirts, Ryan kept a separate portfolio of his airbrushing art as well. He believes it's important for an artist to keep the portfolios separate, and that such a strategy works best for marketing one's talents.

Ryan also recommends that artists read *Art Calendar Magazine*, and the books *The Business of Art* by Lee Caplin and *The Artists' Survival Manual* by Toby Judith Klayman. These sources provide advice concerning portfolios, as well as other aspects of working as an artist.

When asked what general advice he would give to someone considering this field, Ryan says, "Someone once said about creative processes, 'If you can quit, quit'—meaning if it is possible for you to conceive of quitting a creative process, then it's not for you. You become an artist because you can't imagine doing anything else.

"Art is not the field to go into for the money. You do it out of passion, even if it means doing something else to support it."

Ryan stresses that art is an extremely competitive field in which only those with the most talent and who work the hardest survive. He suggests selecting which city you would like to live in as a first step in planning your career. Research the job advertisements in that city and see whether there are enough art jobs posted to make working there a feasible plan. Ryan suggests doing this research even before you begin your studies, and then continuing it while in school.

Ryan cautions against entering the field for the wrong reasons, or with unrealistic expectations. "So many times I've had young students going into art because they envision fame, glamour, and money," he says. "I've had older students coming back to college for a second career and picking art when they have a family to support and I'm very honest with them about the potential for disaster. The statistics are out there for you to research, but I've seen the evidence firsthand. The majority of art majors end up back in college to learn a new field. However, on the bright side, they will always have their talent, their creativity, and their art to enrich their personal lives."

As far as finances are concerned, Ryan feels that your salary can be affected by how hard you work. Freelancers don't earn a regular paycheck and must provide their own retirement plans and insurance benefits. There are no paid holidays or sick days. Freelancers must learn to be frugal and save money.

Ryan believes that one of the best pieces of advice he can give to the potential artist is to become involved in the local art community. This allows you to network and be noticed. He also suggests entering your work in every show you possibly can. These two tips will help keep you from becoming isolated. Ryan says that at least half of his work opportunities are the result of the time he spends volunteering at the local art center.

Ryan also believes in the value of a good art education. He advises that there is no substitute for the training that comes from a university art program or art institute. He says, "Looking at myself before and after my education, I can only say that it was money well spent. A degree is something no one can ever take from you.

"I've had the opportunity to change streams many times, but I can't conceive of it. I love art and love making it—even in the lean times."

INTERVIEW

Jim Anderson, Stained-Glass Artist

Over the last 25 years, Jim Anderson has established himself as a successful stained-glass artist in Boston. His studio on Tremont Street in the revitalized South End neighborhood is called Anderson Glass Arts. Jim attended the Boston Museum School of Fine Arts and the Massachusetts College of Art and graduated with a B.F.A. and a teaching certificate.

Jim's web site, jimandersonstainedglass.com, describes him as "artist, craftsman, architect, and restorer." When did this successful artist begin to create? "I started drawing and painting when I was young," says Jim. "Even in my baby book it says stuff like Jimmy is creative, Jimmy is artistic, Jimmy can draw. It's one of the areas where I got affirmation as a child.

"I found that I really loved the combination of art and architecture, as opposed to paintings that just hang on walls. I liked the fact that stained glass becomes a permanent part of a building—it becomes architectural art."

Jim's designs include many styles, traditional as well as contemporary. He creates hand-painted glass like that seen in churches, and styles from different periods, such as the Victorian, Federal, and Edwardian eras.

After finishing at the Boston Museum School, Jim went to the Massachusetts College of Art to pursue a teaching certificate as a way to guarantee an income if he could not support himself as an artist. During that time, however, Jim realized that he was actually supporting himself after all. He started making windows for people, and it paid his way through school.

Jim recalls being fascinated by church windows as a child, and at age 26 he designed his first, in St. George's Greek Orthodox Church in Hyannis. In retrospect, Jim says he's amazed that it was such a large undertaking for such a young man. Even his established colleagues in New York were surprised that the commission for a church was given to an artist of his age.

The artistry Jim used on his own home began to be noticed and later brought him commissioned work. He owns a brownstone in Boston's South End, which is the largest Victorian neighborhood in the country, with over 2,000 intact structures. He set up a workshop on the ground level of the townhouse, and renovated his doorways first. Other residents of the area saw the doors and liked them, and neighbors who were architects asked Jim to design their doors, too. Still more people took notice, and the amount of work grew. Over the years, Jim has designed more than a dozen doors on his street alone, which has led to additional work throughout the area.

It wasn't long before *The Boston Globe* published an article about Jim's work. Other papers followed suit, and a television documentary about revitalizing an old art form later included Jim's work as well. Now receiving even more commissions, he eventually moved his studio out of his home to a more visible commercial area.

Jim currently employs assistants to help him, and to do repair and restoration work. In the beginning, the number of assistants he employed at one time depended on the economy and how much work he had. He would hire assistants when there was enough work, but would have to let them go if things slowed down. Due to how Jim's reputation has grown in recent years, however, he now has a fully trained staff employed in his studio.

Jim describes what he loves about his work. "I like going to people's houses and making beautiful windows they really love and that I feel are appropriate for their homes," he says. "I wouldn't put a modern window in a Victorian, for example. It wouldn't be suitable.

"I meet a lot of interesting people in my work. Maybe it's because it's an unusual art form, and it's usually interesting people who want it. The work is fun and challenging, and I'm always learning something new. The older I get, the more complicated and sophisticated the commissions get."

Jim is honest about the finances of his profession. "Money doesn't come in regularly, but it always seems to come in," he says. "Sometimes in big chunks, sometimes in little chunks. I never know when or what (it will be), but I haven't starved and I haven't not paid my bills yet."

His years as a professional artist allow Jim to offer some advice to those who might hope to follow in his footsteps. "Follow your dream. Listen to your gut on what to do. Visualize what you want for yourself, then slowly go toward it."

Jim stresses that starting slowly is usually a good idea. In his first studio, he made worktables out of whatever materials were available, using as little money as possible. He advises against spending more than necessary, especially when starting out. "Let your business build up and don't overextend yourself," he says.

Regarding work space, Jim recommends looking into the cooperative buildings for artists in many major cities. This environment gives artists the opportunity to share space with others who are creating as well. It provides a lot of exposure, lets the artist be part of the community, and the rents are generally reasonable.

Jim's basic advice for survival is this, "Just work hard and keep an eye on every aspect of the business, including the bookkeeping."

EMPLOYMENT SETTINGS

Although most fine artists are usually self-employed and work in their own studios, they still depend on stores, galleries, museums, and private collectors as outlets for their work. Others have what many consider to be the ideal situation—a combined working studio and storefront. Still others follow the art fair circuit by packing up their artwork and touring the country on a regular basis, deriving most (if not all) of their income from this source alone.

However, many artists will tell you that any of these options can be risky, with no guarantee of sales. The art fair circuit, in particular, can be unreliable, vulnerable to the vagaries of the weather and the whim of impulse buyers or true art lovers and collectors.

For those who prefer the stability of job security and a dependable income, there is another setting in which artists and artisans may perform their art while being gainfully employed, either in a full- or part-time capacity.

LIVING HISTORY MUSEUMS

A living history museum is a vibrant, active village, town, or city where the day-to-day life of a particular time period has been authentically re-created. Colonial Williamsburg in Virginia and Plimoth Plantation in Massachusetts are just two examples of living history museums. Once you step through their gates, you leave the present behind. The houses and public buildings are restored originals or thoroughly researched reproductions. Interiors are outfitted with period furniture, cookware, bed linens, and tablecloths. Peek under a bed and you might even find a 200- or 300-year-old mousetrap.

Residents wear the clothing of their day and discuss with visitors their dreams and concerns while going about their daily tasks. If you were to stop a costumed gentleman passing by and ask where the nearest McDonald's is, he wouldn't have any idea what you were talking about—unless he thought to direct you to a neighbor's farm. He might even do so using the dialect of his home country.

These large enterprises offer employment for professional and entry-level workers in a wide variety of categories. Those positions of particular interest to artists are artisans in the historic trades.

Artisans

Most living history museums employ skilled artisans to demonstrate early crafts and trades. Some of these artisans perform in the first-person, playing the role of a particular character of the time. Others wear 20th-century clothing and discuss their craft from a modern perspective.

In the stores and workshops lining the Duke of Gloucester and Francis Streets in Colonial Williamsburg, you will find harness makers, milliners, tailors, needleworkers, silversmiths, apothecaries, candle makers, bookbinders, printers, and wig makers. In the Pilgrim Village and Crafts Center at Plimoth Plantation are coopers, blacksmiths, joiners (cabinetmakers), potters, basket makers, and weavers.

In addition to demonstrations, artisans often produce many of the items used on display in the various exhibits. This includes the furniture, cookware, and even sometimes the actual buildings.

Job Strategies for Living History Museums

The competition is fairly high for artisan or costumer positions at living history museums. For example, the wardrobe department at Plimoth Plantation is a small one, currently employing only four workers. Other larger living history museums, such as Colonial Williamsburg, employ more people. A good way to get a foot in the door is to apply for an apprenticeship, internship, or work-study position. Many start out as character interpreters or presenters, and then move into their chosen positions when openings occur.

INTERVIEW

Deb Mason, Potter

In the Crafts Center at Plimoth Plantation, four different potters demonstrate the art of 17th-century throwing techniques, though only one potter is on duty at a time. They also make all the pieces used in the Village by the interpreters. During the winter months when the museum is closed to visitors, the potters make enough items to replenish their stock.

Deb Mason earned her B.A. in art with a major in ceramics in 1973 from Bennington College in Vermont. She taught ceramics full time for 13 years at a private school, and was the head of the art department her last few years there. She joined the staff at Plimoth Plantation in 1992.

In addition to her own home studio, where she teaches pottery classes, does commission work, and makes pieces for display at various galleries, Deb spends two eight-hour days a week in the Crafts Center, and is the supervisor of the other potters.

Deb explains that since pottery was not made in the Village in 1627, the potters do not have to work strictly within the parameters of the 17th century. This gives them an advantage over the character interpreters, for example. The interpreters have to speak as though they are Pilgrims and cannot share any knowledge beyond what would have been known in 1627, but potters in the Craft Center can answer questions that the interpreters cannot.

The potters use modern equipment, but are considering going back in time and using wood-burning stoves and kick wheels. The electric wheels that they use now might make throwing look faster and easier than it was in the 17th century, but the techniques are still very much the same.

"The difference is we have to make only period pieces and there some of the difficulties come in," Deb says. "For example, we're trying to find the right clay bodies to work with. We have a few original pieces on display to study, and you can see the clay color and texture. We've been experimenting, trying to develop clay bodies that are close to the original."

"That's been fairly successful, but we're having a tough time with glazes. They used a lot of lead back then. In fact, almost every glaze was lead-based. Because we sell the pieces we make in the gift shop and they're also used in the Village every day, we've been trying to get away from lead. It's hard to come up with glazes that have the same shine and the same colors; lead has a very typical look. We're using a ground glass that melts at a low temperature, which is a characteristic of lead, and produces similar results."

The potters make ointment pots that hold salves and healing lotions, apothecary jars, bowls, porringers for porridge, oil lamps, candlesticks, and pipkins, which are small cooking pots with a side handle and three little legs on the bottom. They also make three handled cups, because the Pilgrims often shared their eating implements. The novelty of such items makes them popular sellers in the gift shop.

Deb explains that pottery was hastily thrown in the 17th century since the Pilgrims strove to create utilitarian items rather than objects of beauty. For this reason, Deb says, "My biggest problem is remembering not to throw too well. The advantage to that, though, for potters wanting to work here, is that a high degree of skill is not necessary."

INTERVIEW

Patricia Baker, Costumer

Patricia Baker is Wardrobe and Textiles Manager at Plimoth Plantation. She graduated from the Massachusetts College of Art in 1976 with a B.F.A. degree (Bachelor of Fine Arts) in crafts. Her concentration was in fabrics and fibers.

Patricia began working at Plimoth Plantation as a character interpreter immediately after graduation. In 1985, she joined the wardrobe department and became manager the following year. Her office and work space occupy a section of a converted dairy barn on the grounds of the museum. The atmosphere is that of a cozy living room with lots of shelves and fabrics draped here and there, sewing machines and rocking chairs, a large cutting table, garment racks, and a radio.

Patricia's department makes clothing that is representative of what the middle class would have worn in 1627. In an attempt at true authenticity, the costumers provide interpreters with enough clothing to dress authentically right down to their undergarments.

The basic undergarment for both men and women is a linen shift that falls to the knees. Over this, the men wear breeches and a doublet, which is a close-fitting jacket that comes to just above the waist. The breeches are tied into the jacket by laces. Women wear a plain corset over their shifts, followed by a number of petticoats and skirts, plus a padded roll to enhance their hips.

Since the costumers try to duplicate the materials used in the 17th century, the garments are made of wool, linen, and cotton, all naturally dyed. Much of the sewing is done by hand, as it would have been in the 1600s.

The costume department also makes the household furnishings used in the various exhibits. Items on display include the 17th century versions of such things as sheets, pillow cases, feather and straw beds, paneled bed curtains, tablecloths, napkins, and cupboard cloths.

Maintaining and repairing existing costumes and furnishings is also part of the costumers' duties, as well as conducting the necessary research to keep their creations accurate for the particular time period. Because there are so few surviving garments, the costumers look to different sources such as paintings, engravings, woodcuts, written descriptions, wills, inventories, diaries, and plays. They also study the few remaining garments on display in different museums using Plimoth Plantation's extensive slide collection of styles and techniques.

THE QUALIFICATIONS YOU'LL NEED

In the fine arts field, formal training requirements do not exist, but it is very difficult to become skilled enough to make a living without some basic training. Bachelor's and graduate degree programs in fine arts are offered in many colleges and universities. (See the introduction to this book for some samplings of art programs.)

In addition to the skills they learn or hone, art majors make important contacts during their formal training years. Instructors are often working artists with hands-on experience and advice to offer.

CAREER OUTLOOK

The fine arts field has a glamorous and exciting image. Many people with a love for drawing and creative ability qualify for entry into this field. As a result, competition is keen for both salaried jobs and freelance work in the fine arts.

However, employment of fine artists is expected to increase because of population growth, rising incomes, and increases in the number of people who appreciate fine arts.

Despite the expected employment growth, the numbers of those seeking entry to this field will continue to exceed employment opportunities. Fine artists, in particular, may find it difficult to earn a living solely by selling their artwork. Nonetheless, graphic arts studios, clients, and galleries alike are always on the lookout for artists who display outstanding talent, creativity, and style. Talented artists who have developed a mastery of artistic techniques and skills should continue to be in great demand.

INCOME

The gallery and artist predetermine how much each earns from a sale. Only the most successful fine artists are able to support themselves exclusively through the sale of their works, however. Most fine artists hold other jobs as well.

Earnings for self-employed visual artists vary widely. Those struggling to gain experience and a reputation may be forced to charge what amounts to less than minimum wage for their work. Well-established fine artists may earn much more than salaried artists, but self-employed artists do not receive benefits such as paid holidays, sick leave, health insurance, or pensions.

Salaries for artisans at living history museums differ depending on whether they are full-time or part-time. The latter group earns an hourly wage ranging between $7.50 and $10. A new graduate just starting out full-time can expect to earn an annual salary in the high teens to mid-20s, depending on the location and available funding.

Median annual earnings of salaried fine artists—including painters, sculptors, and illustrators—were $35,260 in 2002. The middle 50 percent earned between $23,970 and $48,040. The lowest 10 percent earned less than $16,900, while the highest 10 percent earned more than $73,560.

CHAPTER

4

ART EDUCATION

The old adage, "Those who can, do; those who can't, teach," couldn't be farther from the truth for this particular career track. For the most part, art educators can do as well as teach.

For many, a job as an art teacher is a means to an end. They place their teaching job in a companion role to a parallel or primary career as a studio or commercial artist. The teaching job provides the security of a regular paycheck and health benefits that a freelancing career might not offer—at least not yet. Most states have tenure laws that prevent teachers from being fired without just cause and due process. Teachers may obtain tenure after they have satisfactorily completed a probationary period of teaching, normally three years. Tenure is not a guarantee of a job, but it does provide some security.

Full-time art teaching positions in public or private schools often employ ten-month contracts, leaving summers and several weeks during the year free to pursue individual projects. There are also many settings where art teachers can work part-time, leaving even more hours free for studio or commercial art undertakings.

For others, teaching is the end to the means. For these teachers, their talent and love of art is best expressed by sharing it and encouraging it in others. Although most probably still practice their art, they do it more for self-expression and self-satisfaction than as a way to earn a living.

Some would say that all artists are able to teach, that the ability to share techniques and encourage proficiency is a natural extension of their own creativity. This may or may not be true.

However, no matter what the subject area—art or science or air-conditioning repair—there are certain qualities and skills that all teachers must possess in addition to being knowledgeable about their specialty. The ability to communicate, inspire trust and confidence, and motivate students, as well as understand their educational and emotional needs, is essential for teachers. Instructors also should be organized, dependable, and patient, as well as creative.

THE QUALIFICATIONS YOU'LL NEED

Is it necessary to have a college degree to teach art? The answer to that is a resounding "no." The degree of formal training and qualifications varies depending on the work setting and education level. In many instructional situations and settings, an artist's skill, as evidenced by his or her portfolio or reputation, is highly sought after. Professional artists who lack a formal degree but have made a name for themselves are often invited as guest lecturers to teach studio classes or workshops at various art schools or other settings across the country. But this opportunity is usually available only for established artists. Those who have not yet earned a reputation can still find employment without a degree, although it is generally limited to part-time positions, usually with an hourly wage for a salary.

For full-time positions with professional-level salaries, a bachelor's degree is the usual minimum requirement. But is it necessary to have a state teaching certificate to find work as an art teacher? To work in most public school systems, the answer to that question is "yes"—although some public school districts make provisions to grant temporary certification to noncredentialed teachers. These districts have had difficultly securing teachers because of their location or pay scale. However, this practice is not common.

Some private schools also hire noncertified teachers, but with the high supply and relatively small demand for art teachers, they, too, often require teachers to have the same credentials as public schools do.

To work in most public school systems, a bachelor's degree with a teaching certification is required. In other settings, such as art schools and colleges, community colleges, and four-year universities, postgraduate degrees are required. The following paragraphs offer a detailed look at the different educational settings and their requirements.

Kindergarten and Elementary

Traditional education programs for kindergarten and elementary-school teachers include courses designed specifically for those preparing to teach a particular subject area—such as art, music, or mathematics—as well as prescribed professional education courses, such as the philosophy of education, the psychology of learning, and teaching methods.

Secondary

Aspiring secondary-school art teachers either major in art while also taking education courses, or major in education and take art courses.

Alternative Teacher Certification. Many states offer alternative teacher certification programs for people who have college training in the subject they will teach but do not have the necessary education courses required for a regular certificate. Alternative certification programs were originally designed to ease teacher shortages in certain subjects, such as mathematics and science. The programs have expanded to attract other people to teaching, including recent college graduates and those seeking a career change.

In some programs, individuals begin teaching immediately under provisional certification. They must work under the close supervision of experienced teachers for one or two years while taking education courses outside school hours. If they progress satisfactorily, they then receive regular certification.

Under other programs, college graduates who do not meet certification requirements take only those courses that they lack, and then become certified. This may require one or two semesters of full-time study.

Aspiring teachers who need certification may also enter programs that grant a master's degree in education as well as certification. States also issue emergency certificates to individuals who do not meet all the requirements for a regular certificate when schools cannot hire enough certified teachers.

Competency Testing. Almost all states require applicants for a teacher's license to be tested for competency in both basic skills (such as reading and writing) and teaching. Almost all also require the teacher to exhibit proficiency in his or her subject. Nowadays, school systems are moving toward implementing performance-based systems for licensure, which usually require the teacher to demonstrate a satisfactory teaching performance over an extended period in order to obtain a provisional license. This is in addition to passing an examination in one's subject. Most states require continuing education for renewal of the teacher's license.

Reciprocity. Many states have reciprocity agreements that make it easier for teachers certified in one state to become certified in another. Teachers may become board certified by successfully completing the National Board for Professional Teaching Standards certification process. This certification is voluntary but may result in a higher salary.

Information on certification requirements and approved teacher training institutions is available from local school systems and state departments of education.

Colleges and Universities

Most college and university faculty are classified according to four academic ranks: professor, associate professor, assistant professor, and instructor. A small number are lecturers.

Most faculty members are hired as instructors or assistant professors. Four-year colleges and universities generally hire doctoral degree holders for full-time, tenure-track positions, but may hire master's degree holders or doctoral candidates for certain disciplines, such as the arts, or for part-time and temporary jobs.

Doctoral programs usually require four to seven years of full-time study beyond the bachelor's degree. Most candidates specialize in a subfield of a discipline—for example, European art history—but also take courses covering the whole discipline. Programs include 20 or more increasingly specialized courses and seminars, plus comprehensive examinations on all major areas of the field. They also include a dissertation, a book-length report on original research to answer some significant question in the field. The dissertation, done under the guidance of one or more faculty advisors, usually requires one or two years of full-time work.

Adult Education

Training requirements vary widely by state and by subject. In general, teachers need work or other experience in their field, and some fields require a license or certificate for full professional status.

In some cases, particularly at educational institutions, a bachelor's, master's, or doctoral degree is required, especially to teach courses that students can apply toward a four-year degree program.

In other cases, an acceptable portfolio of work is required. For example, to secure a job teaching a flower-arranging course, an applicant would need to show examples of previous work.

Adult education teachers update their skills through continuing education to maintain certification requirements, which vary among institutions. Teachers may take part in seminars, conferences, or graduate courses in adult education, training and development, or human resources development.

Adult education teachers should communicate and relate well with adults, enjoy working with people, and be able to motivate their students.

GETTING AHEAD

With additional preparation and certification, teachers may become administrators or supervisors, although the number of positions is limited. In some systems, highly qualified, experienced teachers can become senior or mentor teachers, with higher pay and additional responsibilities. They guide and assist less experienced teachers while fulfilling most of their teaching responsibilities.

Some faculty—based on teaching experience, research, publication, and service on campus committees and task forces—move into administrative and managerial positions, such as departmental chair, dean, and president. At four-year institutions, such advancement requires a doctoral degree.

EMPLOYMENT SETTINGS

Art instructors can work in a variety of environments. Working conditions, pay scales, and the attitude, motivation, and proficiency of the students will vary depending on the setting. The following is a sampling of possible avenues to pursue:

Adult education center	Prisons
Alternative schools	Rehabilitation centers
Art schools	Group homes

Private schools

Public schools

Community colleges

Four-year colleges and universities

Religious organizations

Museums

International schools

Halfway houses

Summer camps

Recreation centers

Parks departments

Community centers

Discovery centers

Government organizations

WORKING CONDITIONS

The working conditions that an art teacher will face vary according to the type of employment setting.

Primary and Secondary Schools

Kindergarten and elementary-school teachers play a vital role in the development of children. What children learn and experience during their early years can shape their views of themselves and the world, and affect their later success or failure in school, their work, and their personal lives. Their early exposure to creating art also shapes how they will feel about their abilities when they reach adulthood. As many of us know, a negative experience can create the attitude, "I can't draw." The successful art teacher will know how to instill confidence in all her students, no matter their level of ability or natural talent.

Kindergarten and elementary-school teachers introduce children to numbers, language, science, social studies—and, of course, art. They may use games, music, artwork, films, slides, computers, and other instructional technology to teach basic skills. When the focus is on art education, the kindergarten or elementary-school teacher uses a number of methods and different equipment to encourage student creativity. Young children work with crayons, pencils, and watercolors and create drawings and craft projects. Often, the teacher will suggest the subject or theme for a drawing or painting, or demonstrate a technique for a particular project such as a collage, pop-up, or clay pinch-pot. In most art rooms, teachers display their students' work on the walls and tables, creating a stimulating environment and a sense of pride for the students.

Most elementary-school teachers instruct one class of children in several subjects. In some schools, two or more teachers teach as a team and are jointly responsible for a group of students in at least one subject. In other schools, a teacher may teach one special subject—usually art, music, reading, science, arithmetic, or physical education—to a number of classes. A small but growing number of teachers instruct multilevel classrooms with students at several different learning levels.

As you will see from the interviews later in this chapter, art teachers work with different populations. They may have students with special educational needs—or students with severe discipline problems. In addition to classroom activities, which can involve back-to-back art classes with little time for breaks, art teachers have many of the same duties as general classroom teachers. They plan and evaluate lessons, sometimes in collaboration with teachers of related subjects. They also prepare tests, grade papers, prepare report cards, oversee study halls and homerooms, supervise extracurricular activities, and meet with parents and school staff to discuss a student's academic progress or personal problems. In many schools, teachers help make decisions regarding the budget, personnel, textbook choices, curriculum design, and teaching methods.

Secondary-school teachers help students delve more deeply into subjects introduced in elementary school and learn more about the world and themselves. They specialize in a specific subject, such as art, music, English, Spanish, mathematics, history, or biology. Art teachers may teach a variety of related courses, such as line drawing, oil painting, pottery, and art history.

Secondary-school teachers may assist a student in choosing courses, colleges, and careers. Art teachers with students wanting to pursue either the fine arts or commercial arts as a career should be familiar with choices for further education.

Teachers design their classroom presentations to meet student needs and abilities, often following the art curriculum established by the school board. They may also work with students individually. Instructors assign lessons, give tests, hear oral presentations, and maintain classroom discipline.

Teachers observe and evaluate a student's performance and potential, and increasingly use new assessment methods—such as examining a portfolio of a student's artwork—to measure student achievement. The instructor then assesses the portfolio at the end of a learning period to judge a student's overall progress. At such time, they may provide additional assistance in areas where a student needs help.

Seeing students develop new skills and gain an appreciation for art and the study of art can be very rewarding.

Art Schools, Colleges, and Universities

Faculty is generally organized into departments or divisions, based on subject or field. They usually teach several different courses in their department—for example, in a B.F.A. program, an art instructor might teach courses in oil painting, pastels, and watercolors. They may instruct undergraduate or graduate students, or both.

In art schools or colleges, faculty may work with small groups in studio classes or give lectures on art history or other areas to several hundred students in large halls. They also grade and evaluate assignments and projects and advise and work with students individually. In universities, they also counsel, advise, teach, and supervise graduate student research.

Most faculty members serve on academic or administrative committees that deal with the policies of their institution, departmental matters, academic issues, curricula, budgets, equipment purchases, and hiring. Some work with student organizations. Department heads, meanwhile, generally have heavier administrative responsibilities.

The amount of time spent on each of these activities varies by individual circumstance and type of institution. Faculty members at universities generally spend a significant part of their time doing research; those in four-year colleges, somewhat less; and those in two-year colleges, relatively little. However, the teaching load usually is heavier in two-year colleges.

College faculty generally have flexible schedules. They must be present for classes (usually 12 to 16 hours a week) and for faculty and committee meetings. Most establish regular office hours for student consultations, usually three to six hours per week. Otherwise, they are relatively free to decide when and where they will work, and how much time to devote to course preparation, evaluating student progress, studio work, and other activities.

They may work staggered hours and teach classes at night and on weekends, particularly those who teach older students who may have full-time jobs or family responsibilities on weekdays. They have even greater flexibility during the summer and school holidays when they may teach, do their own artwork, travel, or pursue nonacademic interests.

Adult Education

Art teachers working in adult education have a variety of settings from which to choose. They are employed by public school systems, community and junior colleges, universities, businesses that provide formal education and training for their employees, art and photography schools and institutes, job training centers, community organizations, recreational facilities like the YMCA, and religious organizations such as neighborhood Jewish Community Centers.

Many adult education teachers work part-time. To accommodate students who may have jobs or family responsibilities, many courses are offered at night or on weekends. Such classes range from two- to four-hour workshops and one-day mini-sessions to semester-long courses.

Since adult education teachers work with adult students, they do not encounter some of the behavioral or social problems sometimes found when teaching younger students. The adults are there by choice and are usually highly motivated—attributes that can make teaching these art students rewarding and satisfying.

THE JOB HUNT

Several resources are available to help you locate employment opportunities in your field.

The College Career Placement Center

Career offices and placement centers regularly receive notices of job openings. You can also leave your resume on file there. Prospective employers regularly contact college career offices looking for likely candidates.

Help Wanted Ads

Read the newspapers from your area or from the geographic location in which you'd prefer to work. A trip to the library will reveal periodicals you might not have been aware of—and will be less of a burden on your budget.

The Internet

The Web is an incredible resource when it comes to job hunting. Use any of the search engines available to you and type in key words such as employment, art, teaching, and jobs. You will discover a wealth of information online, such as organizations, educational institutions, publications, and a wide variety of potential employers and job search services, most of which are available to you at no charge except for the usual Internet provider service fees. Most public libraries now offer free Internet access as well. Check job sites such as Monster.com and Careerbuilder.com, which allow users to post resumes in addition to searching for available positions.

Internships and Volunteering

Art educators, especially those hoping to land a museum job, often find internships and volunteer positions the easiest ways to launch their careers. Museums cry out for volunteer help, and internships can be arranged through your university. Once in the door, make yourself indispensable. When a job opening occurs, you'll be there on the spot, ready to step in. (You can read more about museum work in Chapter 5.)

Direct Contact

Walk inside, set your portfolio or resume down on the appropriate desk, and you might just land yourself a job. This approach works best in adult education centers, community centers, and other related settings (see the list under the "Employment Settings" section earlier in this chapter).

The Chronicle of Higher Education

This is the old standby for those seeking positions with two- and four-year colleges and universities. It is a weekly publication available by subscription, in any library, or at your college placement office.

Placement Agencies

For private schools particularly, both in the United States and abroad, placement agencies can provide a valuable source for finding employment. Some charge either the employer or the prospective employee a fee, while others charge both.

CAREER OUTLOOK

In general, job opportunities for teachers over the next ten years will vary from good to excellent, depending on the locality, grade level, and subject taught. Most job openings will be attributable to the expected retirement of a large number of teachers. In addition, relatively high rates of turnover, especially among beginning teachers employed in poor, urban schools, also will lead to numerous job openings for teachers. Competition for qualified teachers among some localities will likely continue, with schools luring teachers from other states and districts with bonuses and higher pay.

Primary and Secondary Schools

Overall student enrollments, a key factor in the demand for teachers, are expected to rise more slowly than in the past until at least 2012. As the children of baby-boomers get older, smaller numbers of young children will enter school behind them. This will result in average employment growth for all teachers, from preschool through secondary grades. Projected enrollments will vary by region. Fast-growing states in the south and west—particularly California, Texas, Georgia, Idaho, Hawaii, Alaska, and New Mexico—will experience the largest enrollment increases. In contrast, enrollments in the Northeast and Midwest are expected to hold relatively steady or decline.

The job market for teachers also continues to vary by school location and by subject taught. Many inner cities (often characterized by over-crowded, ill-equipped schools and higher-than-average poverty rates) and rural areas (typified by their remote location and relatively low salaries) have difficulty attracting and retaining enough teachers, so job prospects should be better in these areas than in suburban districts.

Many school districts have difficulty hiring qualified teachers in some subject areas, such as mathematics, science, bilingual education, and foreign languages. Qualified vocational teachers, at both the middle school and secondary school levels, also are currently in demand in a variety of fields. Teachers who are geographically mobile and who obtain licensure in more than one subject should have a distinct advantage in finding a job.

Increasing enrollments of minorities, coupled with a shortage of minority teachers, should cause efforts to recruit minority teachers to intensify. Also, the number of non-English-speaking students has grown dramatically, creating a demand for bilingual teachers and for those who teach English as a second language.

The number of teachers employed is dependent as well on state and local expenditures for education, and on the enactment of legislation to increase the quality of education. A few states have implemented a number of initiatives such as reduced class size (primarily in the early elementary grades), mandatory preschool for four-year-olds, and all-day kindergarten. Additional teachers, particularly in preschool and early elementary education, will be needed in states or localities that implement any of these measures. At the federal level, legislation that is likely to affect teachers was recently put into place with the enactment of the No Child Left Behind Act. Although the full impact of this act is not yet known, its emphasis on ensuring that all schools hire and retain only qualified teachers may lead to an increase in funding for schools that currently lack such teachers.

The supply of teachers is expected to increase in response to reports of improved job prospects, better pay, more teacher involvement in school policy, and greater public interest in education. In recent years, the total number of bachelor's and master's degrees granted in education has increased steadily. Because of a shortage of teachers in certain locations, and in anticipation of the loss of a number of teachers to retirement, many states have implemented policies that will encourage more students to become teachers. In addition, other teachers may be drawn from a reserve pool of career changers, substitute teachers, and teachers completing alternative certification programs.

Higher Education

Overall, employment of postsecondary teachers is expected to increase by 36 percent or more through 2012. A significant proportion of these new jobs will be part-time positions. Good job opportunities are expected as retirements of current teachers and continued increases in student enrollments create numerous openings for teachers at all types of postsecondary institutions.

Projected growth in college and university enrollment over the next decade stems largely from the expected increase in the population of 18- to 24-year-olds. Adults returning to college as well as an increase in foreign-born students will also add to the number of students, particularly in the fastest growing states of California, Texas, Florida, New York, and Arizona.

In addition, workers' growing need to regularly update their skills will continue to create new opportunities for postsecondary teachers, particularly at community colleges and for-profit institutions that cater to working adults. However, many postsecondary educational institutions receive a significant portion of their funding from state and local governments, and, over the early years of the projection period, tight state and local budgets will limit the ability of many schools to expand. Nevertheless, a significant number of openings is expected to arise due to the need to replace the large numbers of postsecondary teachers who will likely retire over the next decade.

Colleges and universities are a major employer of teachers holding doctoral degrees, and opportunities for Ph.D. recipients seeking jobs as postsecondary teachers are expected to be somewhat better than in previous decades. The number of earned doctorate degrees is projected to rise by only 4 percent through 2012, sharply lower than the 10-percent increase over the previous decade. In spite of this positive trend, competition will remain tight for those seeking tenure-track positions at four-year colleges and universities since many of the job openings are expected to be either part-time, or renewable, term appointments.

Opportunities for graduate teaching assistants are expected to be very good. Graduate enrollments through 2012 are projected to increase at a rate that is somewhat slower than that of the previous decade, while total undergraduate enrollments in degree-granting institutions are expected to increase at nearly twice the rate of the preceding decade, creating many teaching opportunities. Constituting more than 12 percent of all postsecondary teachers, graduate teaching assistants play an integral role in the postsecondary education system, and should continue to do so in the future.

Community colleges and other institutions offering career and technical education have been among the most rapidly growing, and these institutions are expected to offer some of the best opportunities for postsecondary teachers.

Adult Education

Opportunities for teachers in adult education and self-enrichment courses are thought to be favorable, with employment expected to grow over 36 percent through 2012. A large number of job openings is expected due to the need to replace people who leave the occupation or retire.

Self-enrichment education teachers account for the largest proportion of jobs in these occupations. The need for self-enrichment teachers is expected to grow as more people embrace lifelong learning and as the baby boomers begin to retire and have more time to take classes. Subjects that are not easily researched on the Internet and those that provide hands-on experience (such as cooking, crafts, and the arts) will be in greater demand. Also, classes on spirituality and self-improvement are expected to be popular.

EARNINGS

Earnings for teachers vary according to the level taught, the geographic location, and the teacher's education and experience.

School Systems

According to the American Federation of Teachers, beginning teachers with a bachelor's degree earned an average of $30,719 in the 2001–02 school year. The estimated average salary of all public elementary and secondary school teachers in the 2001–02 school year was $44,367. Private school teachers, however, generally earn less than public school teachers.

Median annual earnings of kindergarten, elementary, middle, and secondary school teachers ranged from $39,810 to $44,340 in 2002—the lowest 10 percent earned $24,960 to $29,850, while the top 10 percent earned $62,890 to $68,530. By contrast, median earnings for preschool teachers were $19,270.

In 2002, more than half of all elementary, middle, and secondary school teachers belonged to unions—mainly the American Federation of Teachers and the National Education Association—that bargain with school systems over wages, hours, and other terms and conditions of employment. Only about 15 percent of preschool and kindergarten teachers were union members.

Teachers can boost their salaries in a number of ways. In some schools, they receive extra pay for coaching sports and working with students in extracurricular activities. Getting a master's degree or national certification often results in a raise in pay, as does acting as a mentor. Some teachers earn extra income during the summer by teaching summer school or performing other jobs in the school system.

Higher Education

Earnings for college faculty vary according to rank and type of institution, geographic area, and field. According to a 2002–03 survey by the American Association of University Professors, salaries for full-time faculty averaged

$64,455. By rank, the average was $86,437 for professors, $61,732 for associate professors, $51,545 for assistant professors, $37,737 for instructors, and $43,914 for lecturers.

On average, faculty members in four-year institutions earn higher salaries than those in two-year schools. In 2002–03, average faculty salaries in public institutions were $63,974, lower than those of $74,359 in private independent institutions, but higher than those of $57,564 in religiously affiliated private colleges and universities. In fields with high-paying nonacademic alternatives—such as medicine, law, engineering, and business—earnings exceed these averages. In other fields, such as the humanities and education, they are lower.

Median annual earnings of all postsecondary teachers in 2002 were $49,040. The middle 50 percent earned between $34,310 and $69,580. The lowest 10 percent earned less than $23,080, and the highest 10 percent earned more than $92,430.

Many faculty members make significant earnings (in addition to their base salary) from consulting, teaching additional courses, research, writing for publication, and other employment. In addition, many college and university faculty enjoy some unique benefits, including access to campus facilities, tuition waivers for dependents, housing and travel allowances, and paid sabbatical leaves. Part-time faculty, however, usually have fewer benefits than do full-time faculty.

Earnings for postsecondary career and technical education teachers vary widely by subject, academic credentials, experience, and region of the country. Part-time instructors usually receive few benefits.

Adult Education

Median hourly earnings of adult education and self-enrichment teachers were $14.09 in 2002. The middle 50 percent earned between $9.86 and $19.69. The lowest 10 percent earned less than $7.37, while the highest 10 percent earned more than $26.49. Self-enrichment teachers are generally paid by the hour or for each class that they teach.

INTERVIEW

Mindy Conley, Art Specialist, Grades K–4

Mindy Conley has taught art to children and adults in various settings for 15 years. She earned her B.S. in early childhood education from Vanderbilt

University in Nashville in 1986 and her M.Ed. in curriculum and instruction from Trevecca Nazarene University, also in Nashville, in 1996. In addition, she's earned her Ph.D. and serves on the Education Council of the Frist Center for the Visual Arts in Nashville.

Here, Mindy talks about her beginnings as an art teacher and her job teaching art at Brookmeade Elementary School in Nashville. "Basically, I entered the art teaching profession through the back door," she explains. "I wanted to be a teacher. But upon graduation, I taught kindergarten for six months in a child-care setting and thought, 'What am I doing?' I had always loved art but I had never considered it as a career choice."

Mindy decided to take some art classes. While working on her M.F.A., she realized that she could not support herself as a studio artist. However, she was fortunate to find a position at an art museum that combined her education and art background, where she taught art outreach to children in public and private schools in the area and conducted teacher in-service training.

She first became a certified teacher and then added the art experience while pursuing the art field. When she needed to obtain her official art certification, it was just a matter of taking a few more classes.

While studying at the Savannah College of Art and Design, Mindy taught her first art classes to children at the Jewish Community Center. After one year of the two-year program, she returned to Nashville and found a job at the Cheekwood Fine Arts Center and Botanic Gardens. At Cheekwood, she combined her B.S. in early childhood education and art experience to do art outreach into public and private schools in the area. She also designed programs, taught children's and adult art classes, ran a summer camp program, and managed the art studios.

In addition, Mindy directed an after-school care program at the Ensworth School, an affluent private school in Nashville, and developed and implemented a summer day camp program for children five to eight years old. In 1996, she took the position of director of art for a new private school for gifted children (K–8) that was starting in Nashville. Unfortunately, the school closed after the fall semester because of financial mismanagement.

Mindy started working at Brookmeade Elementary 1996, and a year later she became a full-time art specialist. A new core curriculum was adopted by the school board in Nashville that placed full-time art teachers in all of the schools. Mindy had to take two classes to get an add-on endorsement from the state for K–12 art.

When asked what her teaching days are like, Mindy replies honestly. "Sometimes I think I must be crazy. Why do I do this? But then I remember the good things. It is hard to express to people why you teach when there are some real drawbacks. But we just do. We have to."

Mindy describes every day as different and full of unexpected surprises. She stresses that a teacher must be flexible, and willing to change a carefully planned lesson to accommodate students' needs. Although teachers are required to submit a week's worth of lesson plans for approval every Friday, Mindy points out that in art class the students might progress through a project faster or slower than anticipated, requiring the teacher to revise the plans.

She arrives at the school at 8:15 and prepares her teaching materials for the day. Classes start at 9:00, and Mindy teaches straight through until 11:00. After an hour for lunch and planning, she teaches from noon until 3:00.

There are lots of things that can change a teacher's carefully planned lessons. Field trips and assemblies interrupt class time. And Mindy points out that, in elementary education, it is the children themselves who often present the greatest surprises. "You never know what experiences these children are bringing to class that day," she observes. "Some may be hungry and you get them food, some may be tired so you let them sleep, some may be angry or sad because of something that happened at home or earlier in the school day. All of these things affect the tone of the classroom, a student's ability to learn, and your ability to teach.

"You have discipline problems that must be handled immediately and often take you away from teaching the whole class. Bottom line, you meet your students' physical and emotional needs first and teach art second."

On the positive side, Mindy says that most students love to attend art class. For many children, art provides an opportunity to succeed when they might be struggling academically, and she feels that it is important for teachers to keep this in mind. She says, "I believe it is inaccurate when people say you have to love children to teach. It's great if you do, but you must, must, must respect them first."

What Mindy likes most about her job is the content area that she teaches because she feels that it affords her more freedom than teaching an academic subject. She believes that art is important to a child's development and that it should be part of a complete curriculum. Aside from the actual production of art, students learn about art aesthetics, criticism, and history, all of which can be related to other content areas such as history, language, math, and science.

Mindy finds great reward in introducing her students to new artists and providing them with different ways to express themselves. She enjoys working with students at different age levels, experiencing the diverse qualities that they all bring to the classroom.

According to Mindy, the downside to teaching in a public school system, and possibly some private schools, is an abundance of paperwork and limited funding. As she says, "I love what I teach, but teaching is still a job that involves accountability, issues of testing and grading, faculty meetings, committee obligations, scheduling problems, discipline issues, and extra jobs such as bus duty."

Mindy worked for two years in a portable classroom (outside trailer) with no bathroom or running water. She had to carry buckets of water to a large trash can in the room to use for clean-up. Baby wipes were used to clean hands and tables. She describes her move to a new portable classroom with two bathrooms and sinks as "heaven."

Mindy explains that funding often comes from several different accounts, and it is necessary to allocate funds for certain supplies from the right accounts. She says, "It's a paperwork nightmare figuring out what to buy with what and to budget wisely. Because when the money is gone, it is gone."

There is a wealth of art information on the Internet, but funding in many districts is not available for adding computers, phone lines, and modems to art rooms. In Mindy's opinion, too many administrators view art as "fluff" rather than a serious subject. She feels fortunate to work with a principal who supports the arts and approved the purchase of a clay kiln for the art room. In addition, a program in Nashville links businesses with schools as a source of materials and mentors.

When Mindy began teaching at Brookmeade in 1997, she already had a master's degree and four years of experience. This allowed her to start with a higher salary than someone with a bachelor's degree and no experience. She suggests that, since every state and school system has its own pay scale, you look for information about specific school districts where you hope to work. This information is available through the Board of Education or the district's central office, as well as on the Internet.

Mindy has some insightful advice for prospective art teachers. "Teaching art is a great job and can be very enjoyable," she says. "But go into it with your eyes open. If anyone pursues teaching art because they think it is an easy subject to teach, then they shouldn't become an art teacher. A quality art program should have substance and art teachers are accountable to their students for their learning like all other teachers. I was lucky to be trained in a teacher program that got us into classrooms and interacting with students early on. However, know that you can be trained in the best program and when you actually start teaching, you won't be totally prepared. But stick with it, and find a mentor."

Mindy stresses how important it is to determine what age group you want to teach, and suggests visiting elementary, middle, and high schools to help make this decision. She also suggests that you receive the broadest preparation possible, saying, "while you are in school, cover your bases. For instance, I got my certification in early childhood education K–3, but wish I had done K–12."

It is a good idea to learn how art education programs are set up at any schools in which you are interested. Although you will have learned how to write a lesson plan, Mindy suggests you continue practicing the skill until you can confidently write a logical and organized plan.

Talking with other art teachers in different settings can be a useful way to learn about classroom management techniques and discipline plans. These are two areas that universities can teach you about in theory, but practicing teachers can give you practical advice on the subject. Joining professional organizations is also important. Mindy belongs to the National Art Education Association and its Tennessee branch.

Once you begin teaching, Mindy suggests you always do a sample of a project before doing it with students. "You need to be able to troubleshoot," she says, "and be willing to admit to yourself when a project is a flop, and go on."

A teacher needs to be organized. If organization is not one of your natural skills, be prepared to work on it throughout your teaching career. Teachers also need to be problem solvers and resourceful, willing to tap into all kinds of resources for art materials. "Scavenging is how an art teacher survives," says Mindy. "Learn to look at things in a new way and gauge how they can be useful to you in your teaching. Find a parent volunteer, even if it is just one, and use them. They are great for getting the artwork hung in the hallways."

Mindy believes that a good teacher should never find teaching boring. Teaching is full of surprises, such as visits from parents, the arrival of new students, or unexpected meetings and paperwork. She likens being a part of a school faculty to being a part of a family. The faculty supports each other, sometimes gets on each other's nerves, shares ideas, and works together to support children. And most importantly, they interject humor whenever possible.

To sum up, Mindy says, "Teaching is not glamorous. You often work in old buildings or portable trailers, have limited adult bathrooms, deal with head lice and vomit, eat cafeteria food or bring your own, worry over a student, never have enough money for materials, sometimes spend your own money, deal with unhappy parents, do large amounts of paperwork. But the rewards are something that only a teacher can know. You get out of it what you put into it. Teaching is a profession . . . but it is also a calling."

INTERVIEW

Peggy Peters, Art Teacher

Peggy Peters earned her B.F.A. from the University of Texas at San Antonio, where she majored in studio art with a painting and clay sculpture concentration. She earned her M.A. from Syracuse University in New York with a degree in illustration, and now has a dual career, dividing her time between teaching and illustrating. She teaches in an alternative school in San Antonio.

To become certified to teach in Texas, Peggy had to complete 36 hours of college course work, even though she already had a B.F.A. She was also required to pass a pre-entry exam for acceptance into the education department, and then pass a battery of state exams to obtain her teaching certificate.

Peggy teaches art in the San Antonio Independent School District. She is employed at an alternative school, where the district places students with criminal records, persistent behavior problems, and undiagnosed mental problems. Prior to this job, she taught fine arts in high school.

Peggy began teaching nearly 15 years ago at a special school for over-aged underachievers, mainly Hispanic students with criminal records. She was hired because the school counselor understood that the arts could be helpful for children. Peggy was very successful in the job, and is still known for getting a high level of achievement from her students. She attributes this success to the fact that she knows how to teach technique—how to draw, how to see, how to think, and how to plan. She says, "Art is not magic; mostly it's technique at a student level."

Peggy teaches three classes a day with between 6 and 18 students in each. With a school year of 183 days, she is afforded plenty of time for her own work. In her opinion, teaching is a logical choice for an artist who wants to use her talents on a daily basis.

Although working in an alternative school can present certain dangers, Peggy finds her daily routine easier than that at a regular school. Her day begins at 8:00 with staff meetings or meetings with the counselor to discuss students' problems. Classes start at 8:30 and last for 90 minutes each. In addition to her three classes, Peggy has one 90-minute planning period and a 30-minute lunch break.

Because of the nature of an alternative school, teachers must take extra precautions to check the classrooms before and after each class, to clean up and report any drug or gang signs that students might have left. Occasionally, violence breaks out. Once, a teacher and campus police officer were hospitalized after student attacks, and in another episode students from rival gangs started a riot in the cafeteria.

Classes end at 3:30, and since Peggy doesn't assign homework, she usually has evenings free to do her own illustration work. She also documents problems and calls parents at night if necessary.

Despite the dangers, however, Peggy feels that this job is easier than her previous one, where student behavior was as bad and she had a difficult class load. She says, "I know many artists who teach at alternative schools or in prisons or special schools. This seems to be the preferred type of teaching for many professional artists."

When asked about salaries, Peggy says that teaching is one of the better paid professions in San Antonio. Teachers in Peggy's district receive automatic annual raises, plus cost-of-living increases. She also suggests that, although much is often said about how low teachers' salaries are, we should remember that in many areas they only work part of the year.

Peggy is honest about the difficulties of teaching. She says, "What no one is prepared for when entering teaching these days is how very difficult it has become because so many students are emotionally disturbed. We act as full-time social workers as well as teachers."

Class loads can be quite heavy. For instance, Peggy once worked at an elementary school where she taught art, music, drama, and dance to 15 classes.

The environment in which Peggy works poses its own set of problems for teachers. At the alternative school, she teaches basic art to students in grades 6 through 12. The students come through her class in nine-week shifts, each starting on a different day depending on when they were sent from their home campus (for activities such as drug use or assault). Given this schedule, Peggy has to teach projects that the students can start and stop at any time, using basic skills such as design, drawing, and execution.

The materials Peggy can employ are limited, because she can't use anything that students could steal or use to harm themselves or others. For example, some students use India ink to make permanent tattoos on their skin. She also has to keep a careful count of any markers or wax pencils she issues because students use them in graffiti, marking up buildings and doing hundreds of thousands of dollars' worth of property damage around town. Some students scratch their "tags" into glass windows and doors, the damage from which is permanent. Peggy has had several students who served time in jail for tagging and continued doing it regardless of the consequences.

Teachers in alternative schools are also responsible for following a complex set of guidelines to address problem behavior in students. A teacher must counsel the student privately, document the conversation, and get a written contractual agreement with the student. They must also refer a student to his or her homeroom teacher, counselor, and home team to discuss any problem, chart student behavior during class periods, and call and document poor behavior with parents—all before referring a student to an administrator for any behavioral problems. The average classroom can have many such problems.

Peggy finds that in the poor districts where she teaches, parents are usually supportive of teachers' efforts, but are unable to control children who are involved in gang activity. She says, "It is an unusual experience to try to correct the behavior of a student who you happen to know for a fact is engaged in nightly drive-by shooting activities. If we teachers really knew how dangerous students are we would not have the courage to deal with them."

An additional problem is that many schools are old and not maintained properly so the atmosphere is polluted, causing health problems for teachers and students. Peggy has worked in schools where the air-conditioning system was saturated with mold, or where construction dust and fumes caused entire classrooms of students to have respiratory problems.

Teachers can be subjected to tremendous stress, having to deal with overstressed fellow teachers, difficult administrators, and a high percentage of problem students. Peggy says, "Mainstreaming of emotionally disturbed students means we can have three persistent misbehavior students, two emotionally disturbed students, four learning-disabled students, two physically handicapped students, and any number of regular students in the same classroom. We have to justify our lesson plans with administration for each student and explain why we might have some students who are failing all their classes.

"If you have noticed that I haven't yet mentioned anything about actual teaching, it is because we really get to do very little teaching these days. We spend most of our time documenting, counseling, and disciplining before we can get to any teaching."

Peggy says that a teacher who ends up in a bad school only has to be there for one year. After that time, teachers can move to another school with good recommendations from their current administration.

Despite all of the problems she's mentioned, Peggy does believe that teaching can be a tremendously enjoyable and rewarding experience. She feels that an effective teacher must be constantly creative in managing students' behavior and original in planning lessons. "As all artists know," she says, "there is nothing like setting a lot of young minds to a problem to stimulate your own creativity."

Peggy has gotten many good ideas from her students. She is interested in designing a book of lesson plans for art teachers based on computer graphics, which she believes would be more useful to teachers than much of what is available.

When asked what advice she would give prospective art teachers, Peggy says, "I believe you should be able to do it before you can teach it. As far as being qualified to teach art: If you are an artist, you can teach art. I do not believe in an art-teaching degree. I don't think any teaching degree is valid. You should have a degree in art, not art education. I think the latter should be outlawed. You must be able to do what you teach. I am able to deal with emotionally disturbed students because art school was such a horribly cruel experience for me, with constant criticism and vicious treatment from teachers and fellow students, that teaching difficult kids is no different than dealing with art professors and art students."

Temperament is another major consideration for teaching. You must have a good attitude toward people in general, with a profound respect for the individual and an understanding of human nature.

Peggy warns against prejudging students and assuming that any child has a limited future. As she says, "Kids are guaranteed to make a monkey out of you every time if you prejudge them."

Detached, concerned professionalism is best to serve the students' interests. "Remember," Peggy says, "you are a powerful authority figure put in a position that can create a rebellious attitude in American youth. Don't abuse your position and don't think the kids are your friends. You will serve them best as a teacher, not a buddy; it's a special relationship and must be understood by the teacher or you will not be able to deflect the frequent abuse for which the position targets you."

INTERVIEW

Lynne Robins, Art Teacher

Lynne Robins is a special education teacher at the William Monroe Trotter School, an elementary school in Boston, Massachusetts. She studied at Bennington College in Vermont and earned her B.A. in psychology with a concentration in art. She earned her M.Ed. at Boston College in special education and her M.S.A.E. (master of science in art education) from the Massachusetts College of Art.

In her current job, Lynne works with special education children in grades one through five, as well as with regular education children in integrated classrooms. She is a certified art teacher, special education teacher, and elementary teacher. She has taught in several fields, beginning with multiple handicapped deaf children and adolescents before switching to work with disadvantaged children in the inner-city schools.

Back in college, Lynne changed her major from art to psychology with a concentration in art. She wasn't sure what direction she would take, but took advantage of an employer's offer of partial tuition reimbursement. She passed the GRE (graduate record examination) and enrolled in a graduate program. Then, while studying at Bennington, she visited a classroom at a Headstart program and was impressed by what she saw. Although the program had little money, it had a wealth of innovative ideas. Brushes were made from sponges and branches, and blocks were created from lumber scraps and pegs. The children were happy, and Lynne was so impressed by the teacher that she decided she wanted to teach, too.

In describing her career path, Lynne says, "I am an artist. I kind of stumbled into special education, then into art as an art teacher with various programs (museum or community-based or summer schools) and finally began using art no matter where I was stationed or in what capacity, because it was a part of me and the way I functioned best."

Lynne found her first full-time job through a chance encounter with a social worker while she was working as an art teacher at a behavior modification summer camp. The position was at a campus lab school for handicapped children, where Lynne worked as a teacher's assistant for an academic class and as an art teacher for the entire school.

Lynne credits her foundation as an artist for her success as a teacher. She has worked in Massachusetts and California, in private schools, private programs, and community colleges. She worked with deaf and multiple handicapped children and adults for nine years, during which time she faced some challenging situations. Lynne says, "I'll never forget the day some of the wheelchair kids deliberately tipped over cans of paint and wheeled through them, streaking the corridors with all manner of color tracks. It didn't hurt that they also grabbed brushes and streaked the walls as they went. I thought I would die on the spot."

Lynne next decided she needed a break and took off about four years to work as a freelancer and advertising artist. During this time she returned to school to receive her certification in art education so that she could teach art in public schools. She enjoyed the experience, saying, "My training and student teaching were exciting; my elementary classes gave me a standing ovation and my high school classes were exhilarating."

Lynne applied to the Boston school district as a special education teacher. She was hired to work as an elementary moderate special needs teacher, but found her art training useful. Her projects with students were arts-based and gained recognition for both Lynne and her students.

Describing her present work, Lynne refers to her background as an artist trained in mixed media, metals, textbook illustration, and advertising, saying that most of what she does as a teacher involves the same processes as her art. She sees teaching as very creative, in that it involves working with ideas and making them take root in reality. As an example, Lynne cites a student project that involved studying solar energy, creating solar-powered vehicles, and painting and decorating them. The project grew into an immense undertaking that involved eight adults and over 125 children, and may become an after-school institute.

Lynne sees creating art as a problem-solving process, much like science. Combining the two, she and her students have made artist's books, created murals, and used multimedia. She says that most of the students greatly enjoy working this way, and are usually very enthusiastic about the projects.

A typical day for Lynne involves working with 22 learning-handicapped children during six or seven block periods. Most are taken out of their regular classes for their art lessons, although sometimes Lynne works with them along with the entire class.

"The pace is frantic; the day flies by," Lynne says. "It's never boring, sometimes relaxing, though usually totally unpredictable. There's always something new to do or to learn with the students."

Like most of the country, Boston is working toward new goals and standards in education. Teachers deal with a lot of curriculum change and innovation, which Lynne describes as elements that artists love: challenge, innovation, problems to solve, and materials to utilize. She calls her work "creating with a human canvas."

Some of Lynne's students are currently creating books by using throwaway cameras, making prints, creating chapter heads, writing chapter summaries, and editing for spelling. The end results are bound into hardcover books. Some students work on independent research projects with the help of the Internet using computers purchased through arts-based grants. Others use multimedia arts programs (such as Flying Colors and Amazing Writing Machine) to create individual books, artwork, and other projects. Most projects take between three to six weeks to complete, and most of the work is monitored using the goals and objectives of the special-education law, that have been individualized for each student.

Lynne's teaching day lasts from 9:00 to 3:30. After hours, she often coaches students or works on after-school classes or projects within the district. She also takes advantage of the many workshops that are available for teachers' professional growth and development.

Lynne enjoys the creativity of her job. She describes it as challenging, process-oriented, and unpredictable. The arts- and science-based projects are creative in scope and therefore fascinating for Lynne to develop and implement. The school where she works is multicultural—primarily black and Asian—and she enjoys the challenge and pleasures of working with people of various cultural backgrounds.

The downside of the job for Lynne is that there is never enough time to do all that she wants to accomplish. As she says, "The work is demanding, exhausting, and sometimes I wish there were a little less stress associated with it.

"But working with children and their parents has brought me a great deal of personal happiness and joy. I can see myself working as an educator forever."

When asked what advice she would give to prospective art teachers, Lynne responds, "If you want to teach, you will need to reach down deep inside yourself and ask yourself if you have the stamina, the commitment, the creativity, and the endurance."

She also recommends that structure is important. A teacher should be able to structure even the most creative projects, especially when dealing with special education students, who often work best from a structured base.

In fact, Lynne can offer advice specifically to anyone who hopes to teach in spite of a personal challenge. In Lynne's case, she is deaf and works with hearing students, a situation that she describes as having "made for many a hairy and hair-raising experience."

"It has been a personal journey for me, as well as a professional one— learning to deal with the nature of the beast," Lynne continues. "Teaching has been a struggle for me, because it exposed me to the best and worst of human nature on a daily basis—my own and others'! It will call for everything you have. It will demand that you draw on resources that you didn't know existed—mental, spiritual, emotional. The payoff will come from knowing that you can make a difference in the lives of many individuals."

CHAPTER

5

MUSEUM STUDIES

Most people who work in art museums are, not surprisingly, art lovers. They fill a variety of functions and bring a wide range of experience and qualifications to their work. Not only do art lovers keep museums functioning today, they're the reason art museums started in the first place. To understand better how to nurture an art career in this setting, it's important to have an idea of the origins of art museums.

THE HISTORY OF ART MUSEUMS

Most of the famous art museums around the world acquired their exhibitions from private art collectors, whether through voluntary donations or as the result of political changes. Historically, the principle of public control over art and art collections was firmly established in France during the Revolution: The royal collection was nationalized in 1793 and opened to the public as the Louvre.

In the late 1700s and early 1800s, more and more privately owned collections became available for public viewing throughout the world. For example, the art collection held by King Frederick William III of Prussia led to the establishment of the Kaiser Friedrich Museum in Berlin, and the tsar's private art collection formed the exhibits at the Hermitage Museum in St. Petersburg, Russia.

The National Collection of Fine Arts in Washington, D.C. (renamed the National Museum of American Art in 1980), was the first federal collection of American art. It was established in 1846 as part of the Smithsonian Institution, and in 1906 it was designated a national gallery of art.

The word museum comes from the ancient Greek name for the temple of the Muses, the nine beings who were the patron goddesses of the arts in Greek mythology. The term was first used to refer to institutions of advanced learning and didn't take on its current meaning until the Renaissance, when the first great collections of art were formed in Italy. During the 17th and 18th centuries, art museums thrived throughout Europe. As in the Renaissance period, however, almost all collections were private, and public access was limited.

An exception was the collection of Sir Hans Sloane, which was bequeathed to Great Britain in 1753. It became the foundation for the British Museum, the first museum organized as a public institution.

In the late 1800s, several specialized museums were created in Europe, such as the Bavarian National Museum in Munich and the Museum of Ornamental Art in London, which today is the Victoria and Albert Museum. The first museums to be set up as public institutions in the United States were the Museum of Fine Arts in Boston in 1870 and the Metropolitan Museum of Art in New York City in 1872. The Art Institute of Chicago followed in 1879.

TYPES OF ART MUSEUMS

To understand the professional positions an art lover might occupy in a museum, it is important to recognize the different types of art museums and the roles they play. Art museums are buildings where objects of aesthetic value are preserved and displayed. Art museums have a variety of functions, including acquiring, conserving, and exhibiting works of art; providing art education for the general public; and conducting art historical research.

Since the beginning of the 20th century, art museums have seen a number of trends, such as the expansion of large institutions and the creation of a number of specialized museums, many of which are devoted to modern art. In contrast, a number of the world's largest museums have recently attempted to reduce their size and improve the quality of their collections.

They have begun selling less important works of art in order to concentrate available funds on acquiring works of greater artistic merit or historical significance.

Art museums can be classified into two major categories: private museums, under the authority of a board of trustees composed of private citizens and a director chosen by the board; and public museums, administered directly by the national or local government.

In addition, art museums fall into two basic types: the general museum, presenting a broad range of works from early times to the present; and museums that specialize in one particular era, artist, region, or type of art.

In recent years, costs for building maintenance, staff, utilities, and insurance have escalated, while federal funding has decreased. How art museums support themselves has become a controversial issue. Once free to the public, many museums now charge admission. Membership subscriptions are aggressively sought as another major source of revenue. Most public museums now also solicit donations from individuals and businesses, and vie for corporate and government grants. These practices, while both legal and ethical, affect a museum's choices by forcing it to give precedence to those exhibitions and acquisitions that can be funded by outside sources.

In other words, the art you see displayed in a museum might not have been chosen for its aesthetic value alone, but also for its ability to raise income. Exhibitions with mass appeal are most likely to find financial sponsorship; art that is less familiar to the general public is less likely to be funded.

This cold reality often creates a dilemma for a museum's director and acquisitions curator, but most museum professionals stand by their objectivity, frequently having to defend their independent position in spite of the preferences of patrons.

Natural history museums, dedicated to research, exhibition, and education in the natural sciences, are also included in this career track. In addition to the expected collections of gems and jewels, fossils, meteorites, and animals from around the world displayed in lifelike settings, natural history museums also handle collections that include artifacts from ancient civilizations. The responsibility for restoring and maintaining these artifacts falls to the conservators, discussed later in this chapter.

Living history museums provide artists and artisans with interesting employment. (Read about this popular work setting in Chapter 3.)

JOB TITLES IN ART MUSEUMS

In the past, art museums functioned primarily as storehouses for objects, but in recent years their role has been greatly expanded. A growing number of large art museums try to serve the interests of the community in which they are located. In addition to exhibiting their own collections, many museums develop special "traveling" exhibitions that are loaned out to other institutions for display. They also conduct guided tours of their collections, publish catalogs and books, provide lectures and other educational programs, and offer art classes to students. With all these varied roles, art museums can now offer a wealth of employment opportunities to job seekers.

Art Museum Curators

Curators in art museums are responsible for the preservation of the collection and for implementing its visual accessibility to the public. The curator is usually an art historian knowledgeable about the physical properties of handmade objects. While curators have a general background in the history of art, they usually specialize in a given area. Large museums with diversified collections employ several curators for the different departments, such as American, European, modern, Oriental, and primitive art; decorative arts; and photography.

Curators oversee the collections and work at obtaining new acquisitions. They also verify the authenticity of a painting or object by researching its provenance (a document attesting to the work's previous owners and exhibitors).

In addition, the curator supervises the installation of the museum's permanent collection. He or she determines the number of objects to be shown and decides when to show them. Working with the exhibit designer, the curator also plans how objects or paintings will be displayed.

Associate curators and/or curatorial assistants report directly to the curator and help with the varied tasks the profession demands.

Art and Object Conservators

Many people think that once something valuable gets into a museum, it's safe. Unfortunately, art decays on the museum's walls or shelves just as it would decay on yours at home. Many different conditions contribute to that decaying process: light, variations in humidity and temperature, pollutants, pests, and accidental damage. Conservators concern themselves with preventing that decay.

Art conservators, once known as art or painting restorers, preserve and restore damaged and faded paintings. They apply solvents and cleaning agents to clean the surfaces, reconstruct or retouch damaged areas, and apply preservatives to protect the paintings.

Object conservators help prevent deterioration through a number of steps:

1. Examination of the object to determine its nature, properties, method of manufacture, and the causes of deterioration
2. Scientific analysis and research on the object to identify methods and materials
3. Documentation of the condition of the object before, during, and after treatment, and the recording of actual treatment methods
4. Preventive measures to minimize further damage by providing a controlled environment
5. Treatment to stabilize objects or slow their deterioration
6. Restoration, when necessary, to bring an object closer to its original appearance

Registrars

Registrars in art museums keep track of the location of all the works of art in the museum's collection. Paintings and other art objects are often moved to different areas within a museum, or they are transported to other museums for exhibition. Thus, it is essential to maintain accurate records and files. Registrars are also responsible for shipping objects and obtaining insurance.

Collections Managers

The collections manager supervises, numbers, catalogs, and stores the specimens within each division of the museum. An undergraduate degree in the area of the museum's specialization is the minimum requirement for this position. An advanced degree in museum studies with a concentration in a specific discipline is recommended.

A collections manager must be proficient in information management techniques and be able to accurately identify objects within the museum's collection. Knowledge of security practices and environmental controls is also important.

Art Historians

Art historians research and write about works of art. They may also deliver lectures on art history and act as art advisors. An art historian must be knowledgeable about the history of art, past and present theories of art, past and present ways of making art, research methods, different cultures, and sources of art history information, including libraries and art galleries.

Art historians can be employed full-time by art museums or work independently as consultants. Art historians also work in universities as lecturers, professors, or researchers; in art galleries as curators or consultants; in auction houses as buyers or consultants; and at historic sites, buildings, and monuments as consultants. Within art museums, art historians often work in the role of art curator.

Photographers

Many art museums keep a professional photographer on staff to provide photographic documentation of the various fine arts collections. The photographer also oversees the photography of general museum events and activities. In addition, he or she is responsible for studio and darkroom facilities and personnel issues concerning assistants.

Many photographers are self-taught, while others receive their training in a variety of ways: through traditional art schools, university art and photography departments, and through apprenticeships.

A portfolio documenting professional experience is a requirement for employment as an art museum photographer. Photographers can also find work in planetariums and other types of museums.

Educators

Almost all museums provide some sort of educational programming for the public, which is designed and arranged by museum educators and program developers. They explain the exhibits and conduct classes, workshops, lectures, and tours. They often offer outreach programs to the schools or the local community in which the museum is located. Educators usually possess a teaching certificate or have had teaching experience before they join a museum staff.

Tour Guides/Docents

Although most museums rely on volunteer help to act as tour guides and docents (the two job titles have essentially the same meaning), there are still a few spots for a paid professional. Most tour guides have a college degree in either education or the field of study the particular museum encompasses.

TRAINING AND QUALIFICATIONS

With museums offering so many diverse careers, it stands to reason that avenues of training leading to these professions would be equally diverse. An art conservator would have a background different from that of a taxidermist—thus, an educator's preparation would differ from an exhibit designer's.

In addition, different museums often look for different qualifications. Some prefer candidates to have an advanced degree or certificate in museology or museum studies. Others seek to hire professionals with strong academic concentrations in such areas as art history, history, or anthropology. Most are impressed with a combination of academic and hands-on training earned through internships or volunteer programs.

Aside from professional training, however, several skills and personal traits are common to all museum professionals. For a start, all museum workers need to have excellent interpersonal skills. Educators, tour guides, and exhibit designers present information to staff and visitors; directors and curators supervise staff and cultivate contacts with donors and other community members; interpreters, security guards, and museum gift shop staff constantly interact with visitors; museum support staff must interact with one another, and so on. The ability to get along with people and to work well with others as a team is a vital asset in museum work.

Written communication skills are also very important. Museums meet their missions with their collections of objects, but to do so, museum workers must have good writing skills. Strong written language skills show themselves in grant applications, exhibition catalogs, brochures, administrative and scholarly reports, training and educational materials, legal agreements, interpretive labeling for exhibits, object records, and much more.

Other personal characteristics and abilities are also crucial. Before pursuing formal training leading to a career in museum work, review the following list. How many of these characteristics apply to you?

- Strong people skills
- Excellent speaking and writing skills
- Manual dexterity
- A good imagination
- Creativity
- A healthy curiosity
- Resourcefulness
- Commitment to education
- Patience
- Flexibility
- Problem-solving ability
- Ability to handle multiple tasks
- An understanding of the mission of museums and how it is achieved
- Business skills

While many items on this checklist are natural skills, many can also be learned.

How you proceed will depend on your interests and circumstances. If you are clear from the start about what avenue you wish to pursue, you can tailor a course of study at the university of your choosing. The courses you take, or the degree toward which you work, will depend in part on whether you are a new student or are already a museum professional making a mid-career change.

Traditionally, new hires to the field of museum work have completed a bachelor's and master's degree in academic disciplines appropriate to the intended career. Curators for art museums have studied art and art history, while curators for natural history museums have studied biology, anthropology, archeology, and so on. And although such a background still serves as the main foundation for successful museum work, for the last 30 years or so more and more people have explored university programs offering practical and theoretical training in the area of museum studies. Courses such as museum management, curatorship, fundraising, exhibit development, and law and museums offer a more specific approach to the work at hand. Coupled with a broad background in liberal arts or specialization in an academic discipline, this coursework provides the museum professional with a knowledge base better designed to serve the needs of the museum.

Whatever your course of study, most museums require an upper-level degree, either in an academic discipline or in museum studies, museum science, or museology. An intensive internship or record of long-term volunteer work is also required.

Following are three possible tracks that a student might pursue to prepare for a career in museums:

Track One

- Bachelor's degree in general museum studies, museology, or museum science
- Master's degree or doctorate in a specific academic discipline
- Internship arranged through the university or set up directly with a museum in a particular field

Track Two

- Bachelor's degree in liberal arts or a specific academic discipline
- Master's degree or certificate in museum studies, museology, or museum science
- Internship arranged through the university or set up directly with a museum in a particular field

Track Three

(For the museum professional changing careers or upgrading skills)

- Master's degree or certificate in museum studies
  or
- Non-credit-bearing certificate in museum studies (short-term course)

The internship is considered the most crucial practical learning experience and is generally a requirement in all programs. The internship can run from ten weeks to a year with varying time commitments per week.

Curator Training

Employment as a curator generally requires graduate education and substantial practical or work experience. In order to gain the hands-on experience that many employers seek when hiring, many curators work in museums while completing their formal education.

In most museums, a master's degree in an appropriate discipline of the museum's specialty, such as art, history, or archaeology or museum studies, is required for employment as a curator. Many employers prefer a doctoral degree, particularly for curators in natural history or science museums. In small museums, curatorial positions may be available to individuals with a bachelor's degree. For some positions, an internship of full-time museum work supplemented by courses in museum studies is needed.

Museum Technician Training

Museum technicians generally need a bachelor's degree in an appropriate discipline of the museum's specialty, museum studies training, or previous museum work experience, particularly in exhibit design.

Technician positions often serve as a stepping stone for individuals interested in curatorial work. With the exception of small museums, a master's degree is needed for advancement.

Art Historian Training

At least a B.A. with a major in art history is required to enter the profession, but most employers prefer a postgraduate degree in art history.

Conservator Training

Conservators are a group of highly trained professionals who have gone through a number of steps to gain their expertise. Training programs are few and, as a result, are very competitive.

According to the American Institute for Conservation of Historic and Artistic Works, a conservator must have the following qualities:

- Appreciation and respect for cultural property of all kinds—their historic and sociological significance, their aesthetic qualities, and the technology of their production
- Aptitude for scientific and technical subjects
- Patience for meticulous and tedious work
- Good manual dexterity and color vision
- Intelligence and sensitivity for making sound judgments
- The ability to communicate effectively

During the course of a training program, student conservators are exposed to working with a variety of materials before going on to specialize in a particular area. They learn skills to prevent the deterioration of paintings, paper and books, fiber, textiles, ceramics, wood, furniture, and other objects. Some conservators even specialize in architectural conservation and library and archives conservation.

Training most traditionally is gained through a graduate academic program, which takes from two to four years. Apprenticeships or internships are a vital part of training and are usually conducted during the final year of study. Some programs might offer internships that run concurrently with classes.

Admission requirements for the various graduate programs differ, but all the programs require academic prerequisites, including courses in chemistry, art history, studio art, anthropology, and archaeology.

Some programs prefer candidates who already have a strong background in conservation, which can be gained through undergraduate apprenticeships and fieldwork in private, regional, or institutional conservation laboratories.

A personal interview is also usually a requirement of the application process. A candidate's portfolio must demonstrate manual dexterity as well as familiarity with materials and techniques.

Careful planning at the undergraduate level will help improve your chances of acceptance into a graduate program, but because acceptance is very competitive, it is not unusual to have to repeat the application process. Before reapplying, however, it is a good idea to enhance your standing by undertaking additional studies or fieldwork. Many programs, on request, will review your resume and suggest avenues for further study

THE JOB HUNT

Although formal academic training is vital to your resume, hands-on experience is of equal importance. Not only does it provide a host of significant skills, it also helps you make an informed decision about the suitability of museum work. If you start with a term of volunteer work, even before beginning a college program, you will have a better idea of what career options museums have to offer and whether these options are right for you. Many museums rely heavily on volunteer energy and can place volunteers in almost every department, from tour guide and gift shop sales to assisting curators and exhibit designers.

The easiest way to volunteer your time is to contact the museum's volunteer coordinator, who will work with you to match your interests with the museum's needs. Volunteer programs are usually flexible about the number of hours and days per week they expect from volunteers.

Most academic museum studies programs require an internship before a degree or certificate can be awarded. In addition, many museums have their own internship programs that are offered to full-time students as well as recent graduates. You can check first with your university department staff to see what arrangements they traditionally make. If the burden is on you to arrange an internship, either during your academic program or after you have graduated, contact the museum's internship coordinator. If the museum has no formal internship program, talk first to a museum staff member to determine where there might be a need. Then, you can write a proposal incorporating your interests in a department where help will be appreciated.

Internships can be either paid or unpaid and are usually a more formal arrangement than volunteering. The number of hours and weeks will be structured and the intern might be expected to complete a specific project during his or her time there. Often, college credit can be given.

The AAM has published a resource report called *Standards and Guidelines for Museum Internships*. It covers what museums expect from their interns and what interns can and should expect from the museum. It is available through AAM's bookstore, whose address is given in Appendix D.

Later, when it comes time to look for a job, a successful internship or stint of volunteer work can open the door at the training institution or at other museums.

The American Association of Museums (AAM) publishes three resources that provide essential information for students considering a career in museum work.

Careers in Museums, A Variety of Vocations Resource Report offers information on career planning. The book explains the world of museum work and professional opportunities in museums. It includes suggested educational qualifications and experience for specific positions, information on how to obtain an internship, definitions of museum terms, a list of job placement resources, and an annotated bibliography.

Museum Studies Programs Guide to Evaluation Resource Report allows prospective students to conduct their own individually tailored analysis of how well a museum studies program will meet their particular needs.

Graduate Training in Museum Studies: What Students Need to Know covers such topics as choosing between a certificate and a master's degree, finding an internship to suit your needs, and the practical value of a museum studies degree in today's world.

These as well as other useful publications are available through the AAM bookstore. Visit the web site at www.aam-us.org for information.

EARNINGS

According to the most recent available figures from the U.S. Bureau of Labor Statistics, median annual earnings of curators and museum technicians were $35,270 in 2002. The middle 50 percent earned between $26,400 and $48,460. The lowest 10 percent earned less than $20,010, while the highest 10 percent earned more than $66,050.

Earnings of curators vary considerably by type and size of employer and often by specialty. Median annual earnings of curators and museum technicians in 2002 were $33,720 in museums, historical sites, and similar institutions. However, salaries of curators in large, well-funded museums can be several times higher than those in small ones.

The average annual salary for museum curators in the federal government in nonsupervisory, supervisory, and managerial positions was $70,100 in 2003. For museum specialists and technicians, it was $48,414.

INTERVIEW

Erica Hirshler, Croll Senior Curator of Paintings, Museum of Fine Arts, Boston

Erica Hirshler is the Croll Senior Curator of Paintings, Art of the Americas, at the Museum of Fine Arts. She began as a volunteer at the museum in 1983. Only four months later she was offered a paying, part-time job, which two years later developed into a full-time position as assistant curator. Erica earned her B.A. from Wellesley College in art history and medieval studies in 1979, her M.A. in art history from Boston University (B.U.) in 1983, and a museum studies diploma from B.U. the same year. In January 1992, she earned her Ph.D. in art history, also from Boston University.

For this book, Erica talks about her job as assistant curator for a collection of 2,000 paintings. The departmental structure includes the curator, an associate curator, an assistant curator, and four research assistants and fellows with various areas of specialization. As assistant curator, Erica handled a wide range of duties, including working on the permanent collection; organizing special exhibits; conducting research; writing catalogs, art books, and copy for exhibition brochures; administering loan requests; and arranging for the display of various items in the galleries. Erica also responded to a large amount of correspondence, answering inquiries that ranged from a private citizen curious about the history of a family-owned painting to a scholar needing information for a project at another institution.

As Erica sums up her work routine, "There is no typical day. It's a very seat-of-the-pants type of schedule."

Erica describes what she liked most about the job. "I like working with the objects. It's a special thrill working with the real thing that you don't get from slides. I'm interested in them as physical objects. You gather them together for a special exhibition; you get to really examine them." The downside is that a busy schedule leaves little time to do everything she would like to do. As Erica says, "There's a lot of paperwork. It would be nice if there were less paperwork and more time to work on scholarly things. Research is important."

Of course, it's every assistant curator's hope to move up the curatorial ladder, working toward the additional money and prestige that accompany a promotion. In many cases, a curator would have to be willing to change locations in order to move ahead. But opportunities can be limited, and sometimes it's better to stay right where you are.

Erica explains the situation: "We have one of the two best collections of American paintings in the country—the Metropolitan Museum of Art in New York City has the other—so you balance the strength of being in an institution that values your field against some of the other things that might not be so positive. In other words, moving to a weaker collection to get a better title. It wouldn't be worth it."

In Erica's opinion, moving to a smaller museum with a smaller collection is not advisable unless one is interested in working toward a career as director. A director of a small museum could eventually move to a directorship at a larger museum. However, this career track is more administrative and provides little opportunity for scholarly work.

Although the salary isn't high, like most museum professionals, Erica is not in it for the money. "I could be doing lots of different things for $30,000 a year," she says. "I really love what I do or I wouldn't be doing it."

When asked what advice she would give to prospective curators, Erica stresses the need for flexibility since projects often come up that require workers to juggle several things simultaneously. As she says, "You'll have a couple of different exhibitions you're working on at the same time. One might be coming along in two years; one might be in two months. And you go back and forth between them. Or you'll have three different catalog deadlines for three different shows. You have to write your manuscript and turn it in to the editor. You might get to do a book every five years."

INTERVIEW

Aileen Chuk, Associate Registrar, Metropolitan Museum of Art

Aileen Chuk worked for 11 years at the Museum of Modern Art in New York before coming to the Metropolitan in 1994. She has a bachelor's degree in art history from Fordham University in New York and currently serves a dual role as administrative manager and associate registrar.

As administrative manager, she works directly with the head registrar, taking care of all personnel issues and supervising the work of junior staff members.

Here Aileen tells us about her role as associate registrar.

A registrar's duties vary depending on the size of the museum. At the Metropolitan, once a curator decides what will be in a particular show, the registrar receives a list of the items (sometimes 200 objects) and begins to make all necessary arrangements. Many of the registrar's duties involve shipping artworks, which includes packing, arranging transportation, scheduling couriers, securing insurance, and keeping an archive of all works that are lent to, or borrowed from, the museum. The 18 curatorial departments of the museum maintain their own storage rooms and control their own inventories, but the registrars perform annual inventory spot checks within those departments to ascertain that their records are correct.

"I love my work," Aileen says. "It's varied and interesting. For instance, you may be dealing with very small impressionist paintings on one exhibition, then you may be dealing with massive, several-thousand-pound 20th-century sculptures for the next exhibition. Each show you do provides you with a whole new set of challenges."

Aileen describes one particular challenge she faced. Charged with collecting an oversized painting from a home in Omaha, Aileen had to figure out how to move a painting that was larger than the doorway. She had to arrange for the painting to be taken off its stretcher, brought outside and put back on the stretcher, packed into a crate, and put on a truck. And all of this coordination was done long distance. Aileen had to find people who were familiar with artwork and capable of handling such a task to insure that the piece would not be damaged in transit. She contacted local museums and was referred to someone with the expertise to manage the move. Aileen says that it often takes years of experience to be able to coordinate such a project.

Along with such challenging responsibilities come some negatives. Aileen explains that the work of a registrar involves a good deal of overtime and often can take away from personal and family time. Shipments sometimes arrive in the middle of the night, and works that are being loaned to other institutions must be escorted to their destinations. As Aileen says, "Sometimes you want to do it, and then it's a real plus to the job, but sometimes you don't. You might have just come back from vacation, or you'll be missing your daughter's piano recital, or you have a lot of work piling up that you need to get to.

"But, I've been almost everywhere. Last year, I went to Germany, France, Italy, and Switzerland five times. I went to Japan twice a couple of years ago. It can be very rewarding and lots of fun, but sometimes the demands are such that you're trying to do an enormous amount of work in your office and prepare for a courier trip at the same time."

Salaries can be another downside. "Museum work can be extremely rewarding, but it's not a career suited for someone who is interested in making a lot of money," Aileen explains.

Overall, however, Aileen finds much more positive than negative about her work. She enjoys working on a project from inception to completion, and being part of the overall effort that makes a major exhibition possible.

Registrars work as part of a team. While the curatorial departments generally work within their own areas, the registrars get to interact with the staff of all of the departments. At the Metropolitan, Aileen works with 18 different types of art, and with people who have a variety of different specialties. As she describes her role, "You're the central core for all the flow and traffic in and out of the building."

Given her experience working as a museum registrar, Aileen can offer some insight into what it takes to be successful in this career. A registrar should be very detail oriented and have excellent organizational skills and a good memory. These skills help when one is juggling 200 artworks and must keep track of all details and lender requirements for each piece. Although everything is documented, Aileen finds that she also commits the information to memory.

A background in art is not essential to working as a registrar, but Aileen advises that it is definitely helpful. In her experience, registrars are interested in art and are either artists themselves or have some basic artistic skills. Most have a bachelor's degree in art history. Aileen recommends at least a preliminary degree in the arts to gain familiarity with the field. In addition, museum studies programs grant certificates in museum administration, which is a helpful course to pursue after gaining a bachelor's degree. The Metropolitan takes many interns from such programs.

In addition to education, much of a registrar's work is learned on the job. Aileen says, "There are a number of different specialties within the registrar's office, and the more senior you get, the more complex work you're assigned. As you gain experience, you tend to do exhibitions rather than museum loans or other various tasks that might be in the department. It usually starts at something quite low. If you started with exhibitions, you'd usually start with very small shows. Normally, people work their way up the ranks, starting with exams, then work to loans, then go to exhibitions."

INTERVIEW

Joan Gardner, Chief Conservator, Carnegie Museum of Natural History

An objects conservator for a natural history museum will probably see a wider range of items than a conservator at an art museum. Joan Gardner, chief conservator at the Carnegie Museum of Natural History, works with a variety of anthropological objects including skins, hides, furs, Indian robes, wooden dolls, and feathered headdresses.

Many of these garments and items were not meant to last longer than a few years, but some of them have now lasted several hundred. A conservator's efforts show long-lasting results.

The main objective of Joan's work as conservator is to preserve the integrity of an object in its present state. Unlike restoration, conservation does not strive to return an item to its original condition. Rather, conservators strive to slow further deterioration. Joan says, "We wouldn't take a sword that's ancient and make it shiny and look as if it were fabricated the day before yesterday. That's not our purpose."

If a degree of repair work is necessary, conservators try to use only materials that are compatible with the original item and its time in history. They are careful not to use anything that is anachronistic or that could damage the object in any way.

Joan describes one project that involves working with a bentwood box from the northwest coast Indian group named Haida. When she receives a new object, Joan researches the materials it was made from, how it was made, and the colorants used. She takes samples and then sends them off for analysis to try to determine what the origin of the dye or paint was.

This particular box is badly abraded and broken in many places. In addition, steel nails have been hammered into it. Joan says her first step will be to document exactly what the box looks like upon receiving it, noting where the breaks are, and where modern materials have been used on it. She'll then document the colors, design, and technique used to make the object.

The conservators are meticulous in their documentation, and so will note the exact size and location of each abrasion. They will photograph the item before working on it, during the working process, and after they have finished. Joan describes this part of the process by saying, "What we're really trying to do is document what an object is made of, what we used on it, and why we did it so there's a record for history. We're record keepers as well as people who intervene."

Following this initial documentation, Joan will remove any modern materials from the box, and will apply adhesives that are reversible. The logic behind this step is to insure that if a better substance is devised in the future, the adhesive can be removed and replaced with the new matter.

In the case of the damaged bentwood box, Joan says that she won't try to "fix" the abrasions in the object. She may instead attempt to obscure some of the worst ones so the box looks to be in better condition. While she can tone down the abrasions, she will nevertheless document every step so that the intent of the original item is not lost in the process. As she says, "You don't want to obscure the original artist's work at all."

Joan has also worked with elaborate headdresses from several Native American tribes. The headdresses are often quite large and made with dyed horse hair, eagle feathers, and painted wood.

She has worked with Kachina dolls produced by the Hopi tribes of the southwest. The dolls, which represent different spirits, were used to appeal to the gods for rain or other needs, and as a training tool for children in the household. The dolls are usually made of wood, and have adornments such as bows and arrows and feathered headdresses. Most are painted and wear complex outfits. The amount of documentation that such objects require is daunting.

Working at the Carnegie Museum of Natural History presents an interesting problem for conservators. Pittsburgh has long been an industrial city, and soot and pollution particles come right through the building and settle on the objects that are not enclosed. In the museum's early years, most objects were displayed on open shelves, and have accumulated a great deal of soot and dirt that obscure the colors and details of many objects. One of the conservators' biggest and most challenging jobs is to try to remove the soot without damaging or diluting the objects' pigments.

It is this direct contact with the items in the collections that Joan likes best. She says, "For me, working with the objects is the best part of my job, dealing with the colors and the textures and the research to see what's happened to it in the past.

"It's such a constant challenge (that), as much as I love it, sometimes I get weary. It's a big job, overwhelming, and sometimes you can't really put it to bed at night. I do a lot of reading in the evenings to find out, for example, what the latest feather-cleaning technique is. I go through a lot of journals to find an article that's pertinent. That, for me, is the only downside. I love what I do."

Joan Gardner worked as a science and math teacher and a social worker before deciding to return to school and change careers. A long-standing fascination with anthropology and archaeology helped her to decide which direction to take.

"You can't get into this profession without being fascinated with the objects that people produce in various cultures around the world, and what these objects mean, and why they're done the way they are," Joan says. "They're often so beautiful. But you just don't know, until you get into anthropology, what it all means. Sometimes you don't even know then."

For her master's degree, Joan was enrolled in a special studies program with an emphasis in conservation. The program was divided between anthropology and art history, with an emphasis on chemistry.

During her studies, she was part of a joint program with George Washington University and the Smithsonian Institution. When Joan encountered the Smithsonian's program in museum studies with a conservation component, she knew that this was what she wanted to study.

Joan served her internship at the Smithsonian during the entire three years of her graduate studies. She describes the experience as similar to working a full-time job, fitting classes between her hours at the Smithsonian. Joan received her master's degree in 1976 and immediately began working at the Carnegie Museum.

She has a specific recommendation for anyone interested in pursuing this field. "Before you go for your master's," Joan says, "you have to demonstrate a good knowledge of chemistry, you have to be good with your hands, and you have to be really bright. Almost every student has some talent, in painting, pottery, working with metals. Most people have a portfolio before they go on for their master's."

Studying for a master's degree will teach you theory as well as providing practical experience. Once you have received your degree, you can choose an area of specialization. Joan suggests that if you know while in school which particular area you are interested in pursuing, it is a good idea to find a museum where you can serve an internship in that area.

As an example, Joan cites an assistant conservator at the Carnegie Museum who spent his studies working on many kinds of objects, handling different materials, and conducting analysis and research projects. When he realized that he wanted to work with Native American material, he secured an internship at Arizona State Museum, which specializes in anthropological and archaeological objects. The experience he gained during the internship, combined with his educational program, led him to a job in conservation at the Carnegie.

CHAPTER 6

ART SALES

Art museums display works of art for the appreciation of all. But many art lovers are not content with only the occasional visit to a museum. They want to view art on a full-time basis and own pieces of art they can enjoy in their homes or offices.

Artists do not create in a vacuum. While many do prefer to produce art for art's sake alone, many others are happy to make their work available to the public and want and need to make a living from their work. The artist, though skilled in his or her own particular area, might not be comfortable in the world of art sales. The business side of art isn't always something that comes naturally. But that's where art galleries and art gallery professionals come in.

Art galleries are generally privately owned and are similar to specialized museums in which the collection is restricted to the works of a single artist. Art galleries can also focus on a specific historical period, category of art, or geographical region.

Art galleries operate differently from art museums. While the museum depends on membership and grants to support itself, an art gallery must earn its keep by selling works of art to the public.

Who owns art galleries? Art lovers, of course. You can't open and operate a gallery without having a strong love as well as a deep understanding for the world of art.

Who works in art galleries? More art lovers. But the list doesn't end there. Included also are art aficionados with a flair for selling, and studio artists earning extra money to make ends meet—in a setting where they will be in constant contact with other artists and art lovers.

JOBS IN ART GALLERIES

Some art galleries are small, with only one or two employees in addition to the director/owner. Large galleries, especially those in New York, maintain a staff of 10, 15, or 20 people, most of whom carry the title of assistant director.

Typical jobs found in art galleries are described in the following paragraphs.

Director/Owner

The owner of an art gallery is responsible for every aspect of running the gallery, from selecting which artists to exhibit to designing the layout of the show, hanging the artwork, promoting the show and the gallery, and selling to clients.

Art Curator/Assistant Director

A large gallery could have ten or so art curators or assistant directors. These individuals work directly with the owner, representing the gallery and reflecting the owner's taste. They also work with customers (or clients, as they are frequently called), discussing the artwork and making sales.

Rather than hiring a full-time curator, some smaller art galleries might contract work out to a curator on a show-to-show basis. (See the interview with Elizabeth English later in this chapter.)

Packager/Maintenance Personnel

Most large galleries have "backroom staff," personnel responsible for packaging purchased pieces of art for shipping and who, under the direction of the director or an assistant director or curator, hang the paintings in designated positions.

In many cases, packagers or maintenance personnel are artists who take a menial job in a gallery to allow them to continue to paint and be involved in some level in the art world. If you're interested in becoming an assistant director, it's also a good way to get your foot in the door. It puts you in contact with the art arena while offering you an opportunity to learn. You'll hear why they're showing particular artists, how they're exhibiting them, and what is being done to publicize the shows. It's always worthwhile to know every aspect of the business, and these so-called menial jobs are very important.

Framer

Most small galleries farm out their work to frame shops, but the larger galleries often have a framer on staff who is skilled in cutting mats for prints and cutting frames for canvases. However, most artists deliver their work to galleries already framed, so the need for professional framers hired directly by a gallery is small. But framemakers often freelance their work to a variety of galleries or organizations, have their own shops, and sometimes design and build their own line of frames. (See the interview with framemaker Rodney Stephens later in this chapter.)

Receptionist

Many large galleries, especially those in New York, hire receptionists to greet customers and answer questions over the phone. They must be knowledgeable about the artwork shown and be able to intelligently discuss different aspects of the work. Most receptionists have a degree in art, and many use the position as a stepping stone to assistant director.

THE TRAINING YOU'LL NEED

To prepare for a job in an art gallery, a degree in art would be beneficial, whether in art history or applied arts. But it *can* be done without it. Job candidates are also evaluated on their presence and how articulate and extroverted—without being pushy—they are.

Sales skills can be learned on the job, but a candidate must bring to the job a sincerity about art and an ability to talk about art on any level—historic or modern-day.

EARNINGS

Most galleries work on a 50-50 percentage basis with the artist. But if it's a very popular artist, the gallery might take only 30 percent. The cost of the artwork could range from $2,000 for a small wooden mask to $10,000 or $50,000 or more for paintings.

Assistant directors can work on a straight salary arrangement or, as is most likely, salary plus commissions on the work sold—or even solely on a commission basis.

STARTING YOUR OWN GALLERY

Successful gallery owners suggest that a major factor in owning a gallery is finding the right space. It is advisable to look for space in the best possible location, even though it might be more expensive. The best places for galleries are generally in cultural areas, near a museum, where art is already a focus. Inexpensive space off the beaten track will be harder to promote and might not be successful.

Rent is the main expense for gallery owners, followed by advertising costs, insurance, and utilities. A gallery requires minimal furnishings, mainly a desk and a storeroom. Good lighting is a must.

Of course, deciding what you want to sell is a huge part of starting a new gallery. This is not necessarily easy to determine, since even great art can be difficult to promote. An owner must be committed to the art he or she wants to sell, and that comes from a sincere love of the work. You must establish a stable of artists who reflect your taste and whose work can help establish your reputation as a serious gallery.

Matthew Carone, a gallery owner who is profiled in the next section, sums up the risk involved in opening an art gallery. "The tragedy of the arts is that it caters to only three percent of the population. Now that could be quite a bit, if you're in a cultural area, but that three percent is distributed among the arts in general, music and art, so if you want to hone in on just a segment of that, on just painting or just sculpture, there's not that much out there. You're in a minority arena. It's a risky business. But when something happens to have a magic combination, it's good, and the public responds to it, that's paradise."

INTERVIEW

Matthew Carone, Gallery Owner

Matthew Carone is the owner of the Carone Gallery, a prestigious establishment in Fort Lauderdale, Florida. He handles mainly contemporary art,

American, some European, and some Latin American paintings, and sculpture. He is also an established painter himself and often is invited to show his work at other galleries. See Chapter 7 for a description of Matthew's work in authenticating works of art.

The Carone Gallery is a family business that has been in existence since 1957. Matthew is the owner and his wife is his partner. His son was assistant director until he left to work for the local symphony. Matthew Carone is semiretired and divides his time between Florida and Lenox, Massachusetts, where he also has a studio.

The busy season in south Florida falls during the winter, when tourists are more likely to take advantage of the warm climate. Experience has taught Matthew that the summer months are not very lucrative, so he closes the gallery for five or six months until the winter season begins and people are again ready to buy art.

He has some options for acquiring artwork. Several artists want to show at his gallery, based on his experience and reputation. While this allows him to be selective, he stresses that this is not generally an option for those just starting out. At the beginning, a gallery owner must trust his own taste and try to find undiscovered talent.

It is important for an owner to establish that his or her gallery is a serious establishment. In Matthew's case, this happened by way of master graphics, original prints by Picasso, Cezanne, and Matisse. He soon built a reputation as a serious dealer of high-quality art, making it easier for him to work one-on-one with important artists.

Since many of the sources for these prints are based in Europe, Matthew traveled there every couple of months to meet with dealers to discuss current events in the art world. Matthew had discovered a counterfeit Picasso print, and this added to his reputation and generated a lot of publicity for his gallery.

At the Carone Gallery, a typically good day at work is a very pleasant experience. During the high season, January through March, Matthew begins his day by looking over his show before greeting his first client. Once a client arrives, the two might spend a social hour drinking coffee and discussing the works on exhibit. The conversation will hopefully escalate to the point where the client picks up on Matthew's enthusiasm and decides to make a purchase.

In addition to clients, Matthew talks with artists who want to show their work at his gallery. They send slides for his consideration, and schedule appointments to discuss the possibility of showing at the gallery. Matthew never refuses to talk with an artist, since this is one way in which he might decide what to show.

Even if a talented artist presents beautiful work, Matthew must make an educated decision about whether to pursue the show. Whether the art will sell is of prime importance. As Matthew says, "Each space on the wall costs you a certain amount of money. You have to meet your expenses, and every inch of wall space must try to pay for itself."

Once a show is selected, Matthew begins working on the installation. This involves deciding where each painting will be hung in relation to other works. In Matthew's experience, hanging the art is something that one acquires a feeling for over time. As he explains, "it's very important to be able to hang an artist next to someone he's compatible with. You don't want any conflicts in image. You wouldn't want to put an ethereal kind of painting next to a very guttural abstract. You could destroy that very sensitive painting if it's within the view of something incompatible. You learn this on the job and through discussion and it's a gut feeling. There's no one book that can describe this. There is a sense that one feels."

Once a show is up and running, Matthew begins thinking about the next one. He generally runs a show for three weeks, and then takes one week off before the next. He normally does four shows in a season. After the shows are over, Matthew displays his own inventory, which includes items that he owns and has accumulated over the years.

To summarize his experience, Matthew says, "It's been the most wonderful life for me. I can't tell you how great it's been. First of all, I'm a painter, I play the violin, and I use my gallery for concerts. I come to work thinking I'm coming home. I'm going to where I want to be. I love the artists, I love selling important stuff, I love people responding to my enthusiasm. It's been glorious. I'm a very lucky guy—I love what I do."

When asked to offer advice about his career, Matthew Carone points out that it can be difficult to even get an interview in a large gallery. In light of this, he never refuses to talk with anyone who aspires to work in art, and is happy to let people pick his brain about the profession. Matthew suggests that anyone interested in pursuing a career in an art gallery should talk with an established gallery owner to get a feel for the business.

Matthew points out that managing and owning a gallery is hard work, and that many new ventures fail. He suggests having as many contacts as possible before starting out, and recommends talking with museum curators and directors as well as gallery owners. To do so, schedule an informal interview, and try to get an honest picture of what the profession is really like.

An assistant director should be well versed in art history, which is helpful in describing the influences of contemporary artists. While a degree in art is certainly beneficial, it is not a requirement. Matthew Carone does not have an art degree.

Overall presence is important for working in an art gallery. Assistant directors and directors should be extroverted without being pushy, and should be articulate about their subject. Matthew sums up his view of the skills needed to pursue this work: "Sales skills can be learned, but you must have a sincerity about the work. I always felt that you never sell a painting, you sell yourself first. That's really a barometer for selling. And if I really love something, it's the easiest thing in the world for me to sell because, if my clients pick up on my enthusiasm, they're sold. Consumers are, in most cases, not really sure of their taste and if what they like is good. My clients, loyal to me over a period, automatically become an extension of what I feel about art."

INTERVIEW

Elizabeth English, Art Curator

Elizabeth English, the artist and illustrator profiled in Chapter 2, also worked for a time as an art gallery curator. After handling the interior design for an innovative art gallery in downtown Boulder, she was asked to curate their first show for the gallery's opening.

Elizabeth finds that curating for an art gallery requires several specific abilities and considerations, including an eye for color and design; a knowledge of what potentially is going to sell to the public; a statement about how the gallery is different from other galleries and what its focus is; an awareness of local customer/client tastes and what other competing galleries are showing; an understanding of budgets and local sensibilities; a recognition of how the gallery is laid out, architecturally; proper lighting and view lines; correct and appropriate framing and matting of the artworks; and gallery spending limits.

If the gallery deals in prints and known artists, such as Old Masters or Impressionists, for example, one must also have a background in, and knowledge of, art history and of the artists' work displayed.

In a gallery that shows sculptures, the curator must also have a keen understanding of spatial relationships. Another important asset is a knowledge of psychology and symbolism, as well as awareness of the emotional meanings of color, placement, juxtaposition, and design.

Elizabeth says that a curator must be responsible for all aspects of the show. This includes selecting the artworks to be displayed; framing and matting the art; and installing the works. Additional duties include working with the gallery owner(s) in designing the invitations to the opening as well as advertising in brochures, newspapers, and art magazines—and even choosing the food and wine to be served at the opening. She stresses the importance of each and every element being consistent, and providing a harmonious and corresponding ambiance to the exhibit.

Elizabeth points out that each gallery is different, based on the architectural layout, the art focus of the gallery owners, their customer base, and budget. A gallery of Southwestern art in Santa Fe will be curated differently from a gallery of antique prints and Old Masters in San Francisco, a gallery selling nautical arts and crafts in Boston, or a gallery showing only contemporary sculptures in Manhattan.

Since she chose to work on commission, Elizabeth was not a regular employee of the gallery. After completing a renovation, the owners did not have money left to pay her to curate. But Elizabeth was very confident that her curating would make the work sell, so she took 10 percent of the gross sales for the length of the show, and made out quite well. She also left a stack of her business cards at the gallery and got some more jobs doing interior design and curating from people who saw her work at the gallery.

Elizabeth's advice to potential curators is this: "Always keep in mind that the gallery exists to sell the art, not as a museum to merely showcase it! This means that you have to explain and depict to the viewers—by your placement, lighting, ambience, and mood of the show—why they should purchase the artwork and, once they buy it, display the art to its proper advantage."

INTERVIEW

Rodney Stephens, Framemaker

Rodney Stephens started working part-time as a framemaker while he was attending architecture school. In 1982, he opened his own shop, which he ran for 14 years. During his years in the industry, he did framing work for private customers, art galleries, art alliances, museums, universities, and hospitals. Rodney earned his B.A. in architecture from the University of New Mexico in Albuquerque in 1989.

Rodney has always appreciated the presentation of artwork, studying the different mattings, styles, and techniques. He learned about color and proportion from his mother, an artist, and studied drafting in high school. He says, "It seems as if I have always known about basic matting, how the frame should complement the artwork, correct proportions, (and) the colors working together."

Rodney first worked at a frame shop in Albuquerque. The owner had recently taken over the business and hired Rodney as her manager. He was left mostly in charge and learned on the job.

He also read a lot of the how-to books on picture framing, which were very helpful. The books taught the basics, such as how to miter a frame, or how to cut a mat opening using a beveled knife. The shop was well stocked with tools, so Rodney learned how to cut the glass, to cut his own moldings, to cut the mattings, and put the whole presentation together.

He worked for that business for about a year. When it changed hands and went in a different direction, he was hired for a management position in the picture-framing department of a craft store. He managed several people and was in charge of all department functions, including procurement and expediting of materials, quality control, and customer service. This job gave Rodney the experience for the business side of the work.

When asked to describe his skill, Rodney says that there is a difference between a picture framer and a framemaker. A picture framer will most often work with stock frames—offering the basic picture-framing services found in most communities, such as matting, dry mounting, and basic frame assembly. They work with some ready-mades and also offer a type of custom service.

Framemakers, on the other hand, design and make their own hand-carved frames, with special moldings, rounded corners, and gilding—creating work that is unique. It's considered the higher end of the profession.

Rodney has done a lot of conservation framing, in which original artwork or delicate papers are preserved, as occurs in a museum. "I have framed everything imaginable: paintings, magazine covers, a baby dress, a baseball bat, medals, guns, a beer bottle collection, record albums, CDs, antique rugs, tapestries," he says. "The most unusual thing I framed was a composition of signed memorabilia from the Clinton presidential campaign for a local attorney who was involved with the campaign."

Rodney had gallery space to present the type of framing work that he did. His space included an idea wall and a layout counter or composition table. When a customer brought in a piece of artwork, Rodney would ask whether the customer had any framing ideas or wanted his help. He had several thousand samples of mat board of every color, type, and texture, and would first lay out the matting to establish a series—single, double, triple, and even more. Once the matting was selected, Rodney would help the customer to consider frame samples. He had frames from distributors and a line that he made himself.

Rodney found the creativity to be his favorite part of the job. He says, "I loved when a customer came in without a clue as to how to handle a particular item and looked completely to me for the design. The most enjoyable part was to take something simple and turn it into something magnificent—and then see the reaction of the customer when they came in to pick it up. That was the best part. Not everyone can envision that level of creativity."

The business did have some downsides. Rodney says, "The most difficult part of the work could be some of the customers—customers who would come into the store and ask for the cheapest thing we had. The word cheap to me refers to the type of work you do, not the price."

Another downside is that framemaking is a seasonal business. In Rodney's experience, framing often falls into the category of home improvement, which is mostly done during the summer months. Since frames are frequently given as gifts, his business would do well during the holidays. But since frames are not considered a necessity item, business could be sporadic. "We'd have maybe six very strong months, but it can be difficult making a living doing this," Rodney says. "You have to have a really good sense of humor for the slow times."

Rodney advises anyone who is interested in framemaking to study the trade magazines and learn about industry trends. Publications are available in public libraries and on the Internet.

He also strongly recommends going to industry trade shows, feeling that this is the best way to learn the trade and learn what is happening in the industry. The trade shows include manufacturers and distributors displaying everything from tools to supplies.

The Professional Picture Framers Association (PPFA) is also a good resource for framemakers. Their contact information is listed in Appendix A.

Rodney believes that a successful framemaker should be creative and a self-starter. You must be willing to sacrifice a lot of personal time for business needs. Rodney says, "It's a very cutthroat competitive business, so you need to find your own niche, find something to make your business different.

"Then make a good business plan. If you have to, hire a consultant to help you. Once you do that, find the best high-traffic location you can. That old saying, 'Location, location, location,' really matters."

CHAPTER

7

ADDITIONAL CAREER OPTIONS IN ART

In addition to the careers already discussed in earlier chapters, there are a few more options for those who hope to make a living through their interest in art. As you will see, the world of art can provide employment for art lovers who do not create works but who can offer other services that are of great importance.

ART APPRAISAL

Some art lovers devote their careers to determining the value of works of art. Those who appraise art and antiques are called personal property appraisers; they establish a written opinion of the value of an item for a client. There are certain skills that are beneficial to anyone interested in pursuing this field, which can lead to employment in a number of different settings.

An appraiser needs good analytical skills and the ability to work with numbers. Interpersonal skills are also very important since appraisers usually deal directly with clients. In addition, strong writing skills are needed to compose reports.

According to the Appraisal Foundation, a nonprofit educational organization authorized by Congress to set standards and qualifications in the field, most personal property appraisers are required to have a certain number of hours of experience in order to practice professionally. To become a designated art appraiser, one must also pass a comprehensive examination.

Several appraisal organizations award designations following completion of a specific course of training taken through the organization.

The Appraisal Foundation's Appraiser Qualifications Board has set voluntary minimum criteria for personal property appraisers. The Uniform Standards of Professional Appraisal Practice (USPAP) are the generally accepted standards for professional appraisal practice in North America. At present, the recommendation is for at least 1,800 hours of experience, 120 hours of education, and the successful completion of a written examination. Most appraisers get their required experience hours by working as apprentices with established appraisers.

Since most appraisers receive their training through professional organizations, a college degree is not required for this career. A degree might be a requirement for advanced designations by certain organizations, but it is not a prerequisite for entering the field.

The services of personal property appraisers are used by a variety of clients. Museums, insurance companies, and government agencies all need to determine the value of items they are responsible for.

As more and more people wonder about the value of items they own, and sales of art and antiques continue to grow, the need for personal property appraisers increases. Many private companies provide appraisal services, working for large clients or individual customers. Some even offer online appraisals, with clients scanning photos of items to be appraised. The online auction site, eBay, offers links to private companies that provide appraisals in specific areas of personal property, such as stamps, coins, paintings, and glassware.

Qualified individuals may work for an appraisal firm, but many appraisers work independently, offering their services on a consultation basis.

ART AUTHENTICATION

One of the most important elements that determines the value of art and antiques is an item's authenticity. Forgery is most common in paintings, since among personal property items they are the easiest for skilled practitioners to reproduce.

Authenticating art—and conversely, detecting forgeries—is very serious work, since so much depends on the decision of the professional. Many serious collectors spend thousands of dollars on a single painting, and even the average consumer who decides to invest a small sum in art does not want to be swindled.

Museums and galleries must be able to authenticate items they plan to acquire. In these settings, authentication may be part of the work done by a curator, gallery owner, or professional authenticator.

Authenticating art requires very good technical skills. While there are some basic visual signs that indicate a painting's authenticity, a thorough examination includes the use of forensic techniques, computer diagnostic models, and spectral and chemical analyses. A solid background in art history and familiarity with painting techniques are also needed, as are strong computer skills.

Museum specialists, art dealers, and gallery owners are usually very knowledgeable about the visual methods of validating a painting. They often specialize in a particular artist, genre, or period and are familiar with, or have access to, the catalogues raissones of many famous artists. A catalogue raissone is a book containing photographs of the works of a deceased artist, as well as other important identifying information about each work.

One of the important aspects of authentication is determining the provenance of a painting. The provenance is the history of the painting's ownership and can add greatly to an item's value. A painting or other work of art that has been widely exhibited at different museums will often be valued more highly than a work of similar quality that has not been exhibited. Even the history of the frame can add value to a painting.

To determine provenance, an authenticator must be able to locate and search through any records that pertain to the painting in question. Sales receipts, documents of ownership, and gallery or museum records are some of the materials that professionals use.

Sometimes it is the history of an item's ownership that becomes important to collectors. In 1990, Sotheby's New York auctioned items belonging to the late actress Greta Garbo. A painting by the French artist Albert Andre sold for $170,000, four times more than any of his work had ever commanded at auction. In 1994, Sotheby's auctioned another of Andre's paintings, which brought only $23,000. It seems possible that the earlier painting sold for so much more money because of its history as part of Greta Garbo's collection.

CHAPTER 7

INTERVIEW

Matthew Carone, Art Authenticator

In Chapter 6, you read about Matthew Carone's career as a gallery owner. Here he describes how he established his reputation by detecting a forgery. Early in his career, Matthew worked with master graphics, including original prints by Picasso, Cezanne, and Matisse. During this time, he discovered a forged Picasso print.

Matthew describes what happened: "I'm color blind, but I have become value sensitive. I can see the value of a color, the lightness or darkness, more than a person with normal color vision. The ink used for this Picasso was called an ivory black, which is the blackest of blacks, but I knew that the originals had a warmer black. On the basis of that I knew there was something wrong, so I went to Paris and showed it to a very important Picasso dealer."

The dealer confirmed that the print was indeed a fake, which brought Matthew to Picasso's biggest dealer, who decided that the print must be shown to Picasso. The artist returned the print with the word "faux" written across it, and his signature. In this unusual way, a counterfeit print gained some value, since it was signed by Picasso. As Matthew says, "The fake was terrific. The FBI, of course, got involved with this; they had an idea who he was, but it was never pursued because it's very difficult to prove. They never found out.

"This event came at that time of my life when I was getting involved seriously and it gave me a new level of importance. Everybody started banging on my door wanting me to look at their Picassos. Now, over the years I've developed a clientele that comes to me for particulars."

ART STORAGE AND TRANSPORTATION

Every time a painting or other work of art is moved, it is exposed to potential damage. The same is true of art that is kept in storage for any length of time. Museums often lend works of art to other institutions for display, and galleries transport art to collectors. Most major museums regularly host traveling exhibits of different works, and some works of art spend more time on loan than they do in their home institution. Even private collectors own more works than they can display at one time. Packing, storing, and transporting art is an important part of the art industry since every piece must be handled with the proper care to insure that it is not damaged in transit or in storage.

There are a number of companies that specialize in art storage and transportation. Most are run by professionals who combine a love of art with extensive experience in storage and transportation methods, as well as the managerial skills required to supervise crews and handle accounts. Workers in these companies are trained in the specific requirements for storing and moving art.

Several factors can cause damage to a work of art. For paintings, one of the most serious considerations is climate control. Professionals in the storage and transportation field ensure that a piece is stored at the proper levels of temperature and humidity. When a painting or sculpture is being moved, it must be properly packed and shipped to avoid any shocks that could cause damage.

Art handlers must also guaranty the security of the works they pack and ship. Companies employ extensive security measures to prevent any potential loss or theft of an item in their care.

Considering the number of works in various media that are regularly moved around the country, and even around the world, it is clear that this is a vitally important part of the art industry.

AUCTIONS

One of the more popular ways in which art is sold is through auctions. Whether it is a local auction house or a major enterprise such as Christie's or Sotheby's, a large amount of art is sold through the bidding process.

A successful professional auctioneer must be knowledgeable about art, as well as skilled in auctioneering techniques. Most training programs last from two weeks to four months, depending on state requirements. Some states have strict licensing regulations, while others have none. Training programs for auctioneers include communication skills, the law as it applies to auctioneers, marketing and advertising, auction management, appraisal, and real estate.

The National Auctioneers Association Education Institute confers four designations for qualified auctioneers: the Certified Auctioneer Institute (CAI), Graduate Personal Property Appraiser (GPPA), Accredited Auctioneer Real Estate (AARE), and Certified Estate Specialist (CES). The Education Institute offers designation and certificate programs as well as specialized seminars in various aspects of auctioneering. There are approximately two dozen approved auctioneer schools throughout the United States, and four in Canada. Be sure to check with your state or province to determine which programs it recognizes. See Appendix A for contact information for the National Auctioneers Association and other related organizations.

Auctions provide a number of employment opportunities in addition to auctioneer. Some of these are

- Runners, who move the items for sale from the holding area to the stage
- Floor managers, who supervise the runners, letting them know the order in which items will be auctioned, and handling other details to keep the auctioneer from being distracted
- Clerks, who record the proceedings and handle the numbering of lots and bidders
- Cashiers, who collect money
- Security guards, who watch over the sold items prior to pick up
- Advertisers and marketers, who inform the public about the details of the auction
- Catalogers, who work with large estates, organizing the items and taking precise inventories
- Appraisers, who help authenticate and place a value on items

APPENDIX

PROFESSIONAL ASSOCIATIONS

The following list of associations offers a valuable resource guide in locating additional information about specific art careers. Many of the organizations publish newsletters listing job and internship opportunities, while still others offer an employment service to members. A quick look at the organizations' names will give you an idea of their scope.

Graphic Arts

The American Institute of Graphic Arts
164 Fifth Avenue
New York, NY 10010
www.aiga.org

The Association of Medical Illustrators
c/o Allen Press, Inc.
810 East 10th
Lawrence, KS 66044
http://medical-illustrators.org

Guild of Natural Science Illustrators
P.O. Box 652
Ben Franklin Station
Washington, DC 20044-0652
www.gnsi.org

The National Association of Schools of Art and Design
11250 Roger Bacon Drive, Suite 21
Reston, VA 20190-5248
http://nasad.arts-accredit.org

The Society of Illustrators
128 East 63rd Street
New York, NY 10021-7303
www.societyillustrators.org

The Society of Publication Designers
17 East 47th Street, 6th Floor
New York, NY 10017
www.spd.org

Fine Arts
American Arts Alliance
1112 16th Street NW, Suite 400
Washington, DC 20036
www.americanartsalliance.org

American Craft Council
72 Spring Street
New York, NY 10012
www.craftcouncil.org

American Society of Interior Designers
608 Massachusetts Avenue NE
Washington, DC 20002-6006
www.asid.org

Association for Living History, Farm, and
    Agricultural Museums
www.alfham.org

Costume Society of America
P.O. Box 73
Earleville, MD 21919
costumesocietyamerica.com

National Assembly of Local Arts Agencies
1029 Vermont Avenue, NW, 2nd Floor
Washington, DC 20005
www.nasaa-arts.org

The National Association of Schools of Art and Design
11250 Roger Bacon Drive, Suite 21
Reston, VA 21900-5248
http://nasad.arts-accredit.org

Art Education

American Association for Adult and Continuing Education
10111 Martin Luther King, Jr. Highway, Suite 200C
Bowie, MD 20720
www.aaace.org

American Association of Christian Schools
2000 Vance Avenue
Chattanooga, TN 37404
www.aacs.org

American Association of Colleges for Teacher Education
1307 New York Avenue NW, Suite 300
Washington, DC 2005-4701
www.aacte.org

American Association of State Colleges and Universities
1307 New York Avenue NW
Washington, DC 20005
www.aascu.org

American Federation of Teachers
555 New Jersey Avenue NW
Washington, DC 20001
www.aft.org

Association for Childhood Education International
17904 Georgia Ave, Suite 215
Olney, Maryland 20832
www.acei.org

Canadian Council for Exceptional Children
http://canadian.cec.sped.org

Council for American Private Education
13017 Wisteria Drive, #457
Germantown, MD 20874-2607
www.capenet.org

Council for Exceptional Children
1110 North Glebe Road, Suite 300
Arlington, VA 22201-5704
www.cec.sped.org

National Art Education Association
1916 Association Drive
Reston, VA 20191-1590
www.naea-reston.org

National Association for the Education of Young Children
1509 16th Street, NW
Washington, DC 20036
www.naeyc.org

National Association of Independent Schools
1620 L Street NW, Suite 1110
Washington, DC 20036-5695
www.nais.org

National Board for Professional Teaching Standards
www.nbpts.org

National Council for Accreditation of
   Teacher Education
2010 Massachusetts Avenue NW, Suite 500
Washington, DC 20036
www.ncate.org

National Education Association
1201 16th Street NW
Washington, DC 20036-3290
www.nea.org

Museum Studies

African-American Museum Association
P.O. Box 578
1350 Brush Row Road
Wilberforce, OH 45384
www.blackmuseums.org

American Association for Museum Volunteers
www.aamv.org

American Association of Museums
1225 Eye Street NW, Suite 400
Washington, DC 20005
www.aam-us.org

American Institute for Conservation of
   Historic and Artistic Works
1717 K Street NW, Suite 301
Washington, DC 20036-5346
http://aic.stanford.edu

Archives of American Art
Smithsonian Institution
P.O. Box 37012
Victor Building, Suite 2200, MRC 937
Washington, D.C. 20013-7012
www.aaa.si.edu

Association for Volunteer Administration
P.O. Box 32092
Richmond, VA 23294-2092
www.avaintl.org

Association of Art Museum Directors
41 East 61st Street
New York, NY 10021
www.aamd.org

Association of Children's Museums
1300 L Street NW, #975
Washington, DC 20005
www.childrensmuseums.org

Association of College and University Museums and Galleries
www.acumg.org

Canadian Association of Professional Conservators
c/o Canadian Museums Association
280 Metcalfe Street, Suite 400
Ottawa, ON K2P 1R7
capc-acrp.ca

Canadian Museums Association
280 Metcalfe Street, Suite 400
Ottawa, ON K2P 1R7
www.museums.ca

Independent Curators Incorporated
799 Broadway, Suite 205
New York, NY 10003

International Association of Museum Facility Administrators
P.O. Box 277
Groton, MA 01450
www.iamfa.org

International Museum Theater Alliance
www.imtal.org

Museum Computer Network
mcn.edu

Museum Education Roundtable
621 Pennsylvania Avenue SE
Washington, DC 20003
www.mer-online.org

Regional Museum Associations

Association of Midwest Museums
P.O. Box 11940
St. Louis, MO 63112-0040
www.midwestmuseums.org

Mid-Atlantic Association of Museums
800 East Lombard Street
Baltimore, MD 21202
www.midatlanticmuseums.org

Mountain-Plains Museum Association
7110 West David Drive
Littleton, CO 80128-5405
www.mountplainsmuseums.org

New England Museum Association
22 Mill Street, Suite 409
Arlington, MA 02476
www.nemanet.org

Southeastern Museums Conference
P.O. Box 9033
Atlanta, GA 31106
www.semcdirect.net

Western Museums Association
www.westmuse.org

Art Sales and Appraisal

American Society of Appraisers
555 Herndon Parkway, Suite 125
Herndon, VA 20170
www.appraisers.org

The Appraisal Foundation
1029 Vermont Avenue NW, Suite 900
Washington, DC 20005
www.appraisalfoundation.org

Art Dealers Association of America, Inc.
575 Madison Avenue
New York, NY 10022
www.artdealers.org

Association of College and University
   Museums and Galleries
www.acumg.org

Auctioneers Association of Canada
10440 156th Street, Suite 305
Edmonton, AB T5P 245
www.auctioneerscanada.com

Canada Personal Property Appraisers Group
1881 Scanlan Street
London, ON N5W 6C3
www.cppag.com

National Auctioneers Association
8880 Ballentine
Overland Park, KS 66214
www.auctioneers.org

Professional Picture Framers Association (PPFA)
3000 Picture Place
Jackson, MI 49201
www.ppfa.com

ART SCHOOLS

The following is a sampling of the hundreds of art schools or institutions with art departments that are in existence throughout the United States and Canada. Contact those with programs of interest to you for catalogs and more information. Where available, the school's web site or e-mail address has been provided.

Academy of Art University
P.O. Box 193844
San Francisco, CA 94119-3844
academyart.edu
B.F.A., M.F.A., and M.Arch. degrees offered.

Academy of Realist Art
Toronto Fine Art School
2738 Dundas Street West, Suite 100
Toronto, ON M6P 1Y3
academyofrealistart.com
Offers courses in drawing and painting based on model of 19th-century European academies. Individual instruction in a group setting. An intensive program with a certificate in traditional drawing and painting is offered. Consists of three six-week terms. Between terms, students attend classes three days a week. Weekend and evening classes are available for part-time students.

Alberta College of Art and Design
1407 14th Avenue NW
Calgary, AB T2N 4R3
Canada
www.acad.ab.ca
B.F.A. in the visual arts and design, including ceramics, drawing, glass,
jewelry and metals, painting, printmaking, sculpture, textiles,
interdisciplinary studies, photographic arts, and visual communications.

Alfred University
School of Art and Design
New York State College of Ceramics
Alfred, NY 14802
http://art.alfred.edu
B.F.A. in art education and pre-art therapy, art history, ceramics,
drawing, glass, graphic design, painting, photography, printmaking,
sculpture, video arts, electronic imaging, and wood.
B.A. in visual arts, performance, art history, and theory.
M.F.A. in ceramics, glass, sculpture, and electronic integrated art.

Arrowmont School of Arts and Crafts
556 Parkway
P.O. Box 567
Gatlinburg, TN 37738
arrowmont.org
One- and two-week workshops are offered in the spring and summer,
and one-week and weekend workshops in the fall. Areas of study
include ceramics, fibers, metals/jewelry, painting, drawing,
photography, warm glass, woodturning, woodworking, sculpture, and
book and paper arts.

Art Academy of Cincinnati
1212 Jackson Street
Cincinnati, OH 45202
artacademy.edu
B.F.A. in fine arts (painting, drawing, sculpture, printmaking,
photography) and communication design (graphic design,

illustration, and photodesign), and a B.F.A. with an emphasis in art history.

A.S. in graphic design.

M.A. in art education (summer semester only).

Art and Learning Center
University of Maryland
0107 Adele Stamp Memorial Union
College Park, MD 20740
union.umd.edu/artcenter
Noncredit studio classes in photography, drawing, painting, self-development, music, and dance.
Several one- and two-day workshops are offered each semester, covering topics such as jewelry making, flower arranging, and silk painting. All classes run during the spring, summer, and fall semesters.

Art Institute of Boston
Lesley University
700 Beacon Street
Boston, MA 02215
http://web.lesley.edu/aib
B.F.A. in illustration, graphic design, fine art, photography, or a combined program in illustration/fine art, illustration/animation, or design/illustration.
M.F.A. in visual arts.
Dual degree B.F.A./M.Ed. in visual art education for initial license as teacher of visual art (grades Pre-K–8 or 5–12).
Diploma program in fine arts or photography—three-year, studio-intensive program for students with degrees in other fields.

Art Institute of California—Orange County
3601 West Sunflower Avenue
Santa Ana, CA 92704-9888
aicaoc.artinstitutes.edu
A.S. in graphic design and interactive media design.
B.S. in graphic design, interactive media design, interior design, and media arts and animation.

Art Students League of New York
215 West 57th Street
New York, NY 10019
theartstudentsleague.org
Classes in drawing, painting, combined media, printmaking, sculpture/carving, and metal sculpture. Morning, afternoon, evening, and weekend classes are available.

Atlanta College of Art/Savannah College of Art and Design
Woodruff Arts Center
1280 Peachtree Street NE
Atlanta, GA 30309
www.aca.edu
B.F.A. programs in communication design, drawing, electronic arts, interior design, painting, photography, printmaking, and sculpture.

Atlin Art Centre
Monarch Mountain
P.O. Box 207
Atlin, British Columbia V0W 1A0
atlinart.com
Offers three-week summer art courses in visual arts (painting, sculpting, photography, and designing in the material arts) from intermediate to advanced.

Augusta State University
Fine Arts Department
2500 Walton Way
Augusta, GA 30904
aug.edu
B.A. and B.F.A. programs with concentrations in 3-D, 2-D, or general art.
Courses offered in drawing, painting, printmaking, high and low and primitive fired ceramics, casting, carving, installation, and survey and focus and contemporary art histories and art education.

Bard Graduate Center for Studies in the Decorative Arts
18 West 86th Street
New York, NY 10024
bgc.bard.edu
M.A. and Ph.D. in American design and culture, garden history and
    landscape studies, museum history, and practice.

Boston University
College of Fine Arts/School of Visual Arts
855 Commonwealth Avenue
Boston, MA 02215
bu.edu/cfa
B.F.A. in painting, sculpture, graphic design, and art education.
M.F.A. in art education, studio teaching, graphic design, and painting
    and sculpture.

Brookfield Craft Center
P.O. Box 122
Brookfield, CT 06804
brookfieldcraftcenter.org
Nonacademic school for fine craftsmanship. Offers over four hundred
    classes and workshops with the nation's top artists/craftsmen.

California College of the Arts
1111 8th Street
San Francisco, CA 94107-2247
cca.edu
Undergraduate and graduate programs in architecture, fine arts,
    jewelry/metal, sculpture, textiles, graphic design, curatorial practice,
    and visual criticism.

California Institute of the Arts
24700 McBean Parkway
Valencia, CA 91355-2397
calarts.edu
Programs in art, critical studies, dance, film/video, music, and theatre.
B.F.A. in character animation, music technology, and musical arts.
M.F.A. in writing, film directing, composition new media, performing/
    composing, directing, and producing.

Centre des Metiers du Verre du Quebec
1200, rue Mill
Montreal, QC H3K 2B3
Canada
espaceverre.qc.ca
Glass art studio offering academic courses, workshops, studio rental, exhibitions, and general information on glass and glass artists from Quebec, Canada.

Claremont Graduate University
School of the Arts and Humanities
121 East 10th Street
Claremont, CA 91711
cgu.edu
M.F.A. in digital media, drawing, installation, multimedia, new genre, painting, performance, photography, sculpture.

Cleveland Institute of Art
University Circle
11141 East Boulevard
Cleveland, OH 44106
cia.edu
B.F.A. in 17 majors among the following areas: design and material culture, visual arts and technologies, integrated media, and liberal arts (visual culture: theory and history).
M.F.A. in medical illustration and visual arts.

The College of New Jersey
Department of Art
School of Art, Media, and Music
Music Building
7718 Pennington Road
Ewing, NJ 08628
tcnj.edu
B.F.A. in fine arts, graphic design, and digital arts.
B.A. in art education and art history.

College for Creative Studies
201 East Kirby Street
Detroit, MI 48202-4034
ccscad.edu
B.F.A. degree in 17 majors in five departments: graphic communication, crafts, fine arts, photography, and industrial design.

Columbus College of Art and Design
107 North Ninth Street
Columbus, OH 43215
ccad.edu
B.F.A. in advertising and graphic design, fashion design, fine arts (including painting, drawing, ceramics, sculpture, printmaking, and glassblowing), illustration, industrial design, interior design, and media studies (encompassing animation, computer animation, digital multimedia, film, photography, and video).

Contemporary Artists Center
Historic Beaver Mill
189 Beaver Street
North Adams, MA 01247
thecac.org
The Contemporary Artists Center is a not-for-profit summer artists' studio that encourages the production of painting, sculpture, drawing, printmaking, photography, and mixed media art.

Cooper Union School of Art
30 Cooper Square
New York, NY 10003
cooper.edu
B.F.A. with concentrations in drawing, graphic design, painting, photography, printmaking, and sculpture.

Corcoran School of Art
500 17th Street NW
Washington, DC 20006-4804
corcoran.edu

B.F.A. in fine art, fine art photography, photojournalism, graphic design, and digital media design.

A.F.A. in digital media design, fine art, graphic design, and photography.

M.A. in interior design and history of decorative arts.

M.A. in art education.

Dodge Stained Glass Studio
1021 Route 82
Hopewell Junction, NY 12533
dodgestudio.com

Offers basic and intermediate classes in Tiffany stained glass technique, as well as classes in lampworking (bead making), and fusing and slumping glass.

Haliburton School of Fine Arts
Fleming College
Haliburton Campus
P.O. Box 839
Haliburton, Ontario K0M 1S0
flemingc.on.ca/HSTA

Includes programs in Arts and Heritage, in the following areas: artist blacksmith, ceramics, collections conservation and management, expressive arts, glassblowing, jewelry essentials, museum management and curatorship, photo arts, sculpture, textile surface design, drawing and painting, and visual and creative arts.

Full-time and part-time courses available; certificates offered in some areas.

Herron School of Art
Indiana University Purdue University
735 West New York Street
Indianapolis, IN 46202
herron.iupui.edu

B.A., B.F.A., B.A.E., M.A.E., and M.F.A. degrees in fine arts, visual communication, art education, and art history.

Indianapolis Art Center
820 East 67th Street
Indianapolis, IN 46220
indplsartcenter.org

A nonprofit, community-based art education facility offering over
200 classes in each of three terms (fall, spring, and summer)
annually. A variety of media including ceramics, watercolor painting,
oil painting, metalsmithing, computer art, stone carving,
photography, printmaking, drawing, and woodworking are covered.
Classes also available for children, aged 4 to 18.

Inspiration Farm
Gossamer Glass Studios
619 East Laurel Road
Bellingham, WA 98226
inspirationfarm.com
Summer glass workshops

Johnson Atelier Sculpture Foundation Studio
60 Sculptors Way
Mercerville, NJ 08619
atelier.org
Serves sculptors and artists worldwide through educational programs,
a fine art foundry, and supplies.

Kansas City Art Institute
4415 Warwick Boulevard
Kansas City, MO 64111
kcai.edu
B.F.A. in animation, art history, ceramics, fiber, graphic design,
interdisciplinary arts, new media, painting, photography,
printmaking, sculpture, and studio art in creative writing.

Kendal College of Art and Design
Ferris State University
17 Fountain Street
Grand Rapids, MI 49503-3102
kcad.edu
B.F.A. in art education, fine arts, furniture design, illustration, industrial
design, interior design, metals/jewelry design, and visual
communications.

B.S. in art history (academic and studio).

M.F.A. in fine art.

Certification in art education.

Kent State University

School of Art

Kent, OH 44242-0001

http://dept.kent.edu/art/flash_content.html

B.A., B.F.A., M.A., and M.F.A. in art education, art history, crafts, and fine arts.

Loyola Marymount University

Department of Art and Art History

Westchester Campus

1 LMU Drive

Los Angeles, CA 90045

lmu.edu/colleges/cfa/art/index.html

B.A. in art history.

B.F.A. in studio arts with a concentration in fine arts, graphic design, multimedia, and art education.

Maine College of Art

97 Spring Street

Portland, ME 04101

meca.edu

B.F.A. in art education, graphic design, ceramics, illustration, metalsmithing and jewelry, new media, painting, photography, printmaking, and sculpture.

M.F.A. in studio arts.

Memphis College of Art

Overton Park

1930 Poplar Avenue

Memphis, TN 38104-2764

mca.edu

B.F.A. and M.F.A. degrees in design and fine arts.

Mendocino Art Center
45200 Little Lake Street
P.O. Box 756
Mendocino, CA 95460
mendocinoartcenter.org
An educational, exhibition, and resource center for the visual and
performing arts. Offers weeklong and weekend workshops in four
major areas: fine arts, jewelry/metal arts, ceramics, and textiles.

Milwaukee Institute of Art and Design
273 East Erie Street
Milwaukee, WI 53202
miad.edu
B.F.A. in communication design, drawing, illustration, industrial design,
interior architecture and design, integrated fine arts, painting,
photography, printmaking, and sculpture.

Minneapolis College of Art and Design
2501 Stevens Avenue
Minneapolis, MN 55413
mcad.edu
B.F.A. in advertising, animation, comic art, drawing, filmmaking, fine
arts studio, furniture design, graphic design, illustration, interactive
media, painting, photography, print paper book, and sculpture.
B.S. and M.F.A programs.

Montserrat College of Art
23 Essex Street
P.O. Box 26
Beverly, MA 01915
montserrat.edu
B.F.A. and nondegree programs in painting, drawing, printmaking,
photography, sculpture, graphic design, illustration, and art teacher
certification.

Moore College of Art and Design
20th Street and the Parkway
Philadelphia, PA 19103-1179
moore.edu
Fashion design, communication arts—graphic design, illustration, and
fashion illustration—fine arts 2-D, fine arts 3-D, interior design and
textile design, and teacher certification.

More Fire Glass Studio
80 Rockwood Place
Rochester, NY 14610
www2.rpa.net/~morefire/
Offers evening classes, weekend workshops, and intensives in
glassblowing, casting, flameworking, beadmaking, and sculpture.

The New England School of Art and Design at Suffolk University
81 Arlington Street
Boston, MA 02116
suffolk.edu/nesad/
B.F.A. in graphic design, interior design, and fine arts.
M.A. in graphic design and interior design.
Certificate in graphic design.

New Orleans School of GlassWorks and Printmaking Studio
727 Magazine Street
New Orleans, LA 70130
neworleansglassworks.com
A nonprofit school specializing in handblown glass and printmaking.

New World School of the Arts
25 NE Second Street
Miami, FL 33132
mdc.edu/nwsa
The school offers a University of Florida B.F.A. in art and design.

New York Studio School of Drawing, Painting, and Sculpture
8 West Eighth Street
New York, NY 10011
nyss.org

M.F.A. in fine arts.

The 92nd Street Y School of the Arts
1395 Lexington Avenue
New York, NY 10128
92y.org
Offers a wide variety of courses in fine arts, photography, ceramics, and
    jewelry for children, teens, and adults. Professional artists provide
    individual instruction in small group settings.

North Seattle Community College
Art Department
9600 College Way North
Seattle, WA 98103
northseattle.edu
A.F.A. degree and nondegree courses; also offers a more specialized
    A.F.A. and C.F.A. program.

Northwest College of Art
16301 Creative Drive NE
Poulsbo, WA 98370
nca.edu
A 32-month B.F.A. degree program is offered in visual communication
    with majors in graphic design and fine arts.

Nova Scotia College of Art and Design
NSCAD University
5163 Duke Street
Halifax, Nova Scotia B3J 3J6
nscad.ns.ca
B.A. in visual arts with optional major in art history.
B.F.A. with majors in ceramics, film, fine art, jewelry design and
    metalsmithing, media arts, photography, and textiles.
Bachelor of Design degree with a major in graphic design.
M.F.A. degree also offered.

Otis College of Art and Design
9045 Lincoln Boulevard
Los Angeles, CA 90045
otis.edu

B.F.A. in painting and sculpture, new genres, and photography. M.F.A. degree also offered.

Pacific Northwest College of Art
1241 NW Johnson Street
Portland, OR 97209
pnca.edu
B.F.A. in communication design, illustration, intermedia, painting, photography, printmaking, and sculpture.

Paier College of Art, Inc.
20 Gorham Avenue
Hamden, CT 06514-3902
paierart.com
B.F.A. in fine arts, graphic design, photography, illustration, and interior design.

Parsons School of Design
66 Fifth Avenue
New York, NY 10011
parsons.edu
Associate's, bachelor's, and master's degrees in fine arts, graphic design, interior design, illustration, photography, and architecture.

Penland School of Crafts
P.O. Box 37
Penland, NC 28765
penland.org
One-, two-, and eight-week workshops in books and printing, clay, drawing, glass, iron, metals, photography, printmaking, textiles, and wood. The school also sponsors artists' residencies, educational outreach programs, and a craft gallery that's open to the public.

Pennsylvania Academy of the Fine Arts
118 North Broad Street
Philadelphia, PA 19102
pafa.org

B.F.A., M.F.A., certificate, and post-baccalaureate programs in drawing,
   painting, sculpture, and printmaking.

Pennsylvania College of Art and Design
204 North Prince Street
P.O. Box 59
Lancaster, PA 17608-0059
pcad.edu
B.F.A. in graphic arts, fine art, illustration, and photography.

Peters Valley Craft Center
19 Kuhn Road
Layton, NJ 07851
pvcrafts.org
Offers training in blacksmithing, ceramics, desktop publishing, fiber,
   fine metals, interior design, photography, weaving, and
   woodworking.

Pratt Fine Arts Center
1902 South Main Street
Seattle, WA 98144
pratt.org
Studios include a hot-and-warm shop in glass, a sculpture studio, a
   jewelry/metalsmithing studio, and a printmaking/painting studio.

Pratt Institute
200 Willoughby Avenue
Brooklyn, NY 11205
pratt.edu
Undergraduate and graduate degrees in art, design, and architecture.

Rhode Island School of Design
Two College Street
Providence, RI 02903
risd.edu
Undergraduate degrees offered in 16 majors, and graduate degrees
   offered in 17 majors.

Ringling School of Art and Design
2700 North Tamiami Trail
Sarasota, FL 34234-5895
rsad.edu
B.F.A. in computer animation, fine arts, graphic design, illustration, interior design, and photography and digital imaging.

Rochester Institute of Technology
College of Imaging Arts and Sciences
One Lomb Memorial Drive
Rochester, NY 14623-5603
rit.edu
School of Art and Design: art education, graphic design, computer graphic design, interior design, industrial design, illustration, medical illustration, painting, and printmaking.
School of American Crafts: ceramics and ceramic sculpture, metalcrafts and jewelry, woodworking and furniture design, weaving and textile design, and glass work.

San Francisco Art Institute
800 Chestnut Street
San Francisco, CA 94133
www.sfai.edu
B.F.A. and M.F.A. in film, painting, new genres, photography, printmaking, and sculpture/ceramics.

Santa Cruz Mountains Art Center
9341 Mill Street
Ben Lomond, CA 95005
mountainartcenter.org
Workshops in life drawing, watercolors, arts for children, ceramics, enameling, jewelry, moldmaking, and a broad range of media.

School of Art, Design, and Art History
San Diego State University
5500 Campanile Drive
San Diego, CA 92182-4805
http://psfa.sdsu.edu/schools/art_design_ah.html

B.A. in graphic design, interior design, multimedia, painting, printmaking, sculpture, applied design (ceramics, furniture, jewelry and metalsmithing, textiles), art history, and studio art.
M.A. and M.F.A. also offered.

School of the Art Institute of Chicago
37 South Wabash Avenue
Chicago, IL 60603
artic.edu/saic/
B.A. in visual and critical studies.
B.F.A. in studio, writing, art education, and art history.
B.I.A. (bachelor of interior architecture) also offered.
M.F.A. in studio, writing, and modern art theory, history, and criticism.
M.A. in art education, art therapy, and arts administration.

School of the Museum of Fine Arts
230 The Fenway
Boston, MA 02115
smfa.edu
B.F.A. and B.F.A. in art education.
M.F.A. and M.F.A. in teaching in art education.
Diploma program is also offered.

School of Visual Arts
SVA Galleries
209 East 23rd Street
New York, NY 10010-3994
schoolofvisualarts.edu
B.F.A. in advertising, animation, art education, art therapy, cartooning, computer art, film, fine arts, graphic design, illustration, interior design, photography, and video.
M.F.A. in fine arts, illustration, computer art, photography, art criticism, writing, art education, and art therapy.

Seattle Academy of Fine Art
1501 10th Avenue East
Seattle, WA 98102
seattlefineart.org

Traditional training in painting and drawing for contemporary artists. Classes are held in ten-week sessions, weeklong technical intensives, and weekend workshops. Includes courses in figure drawing and painting, realist drawing, portrait, color theory, perspective, still-life drawing and painting, and classes that introduce students to different media such as oil, watercolor, pastel, and color pencil.

Sheridan College
School of Animation Arts and Design
1430 Trafalgar Road
Oakville, ON L6H 2L1
Canada
www1.sheridaninstitute.ca
B.A., B.A.A., and B.D. degrees offered in 24 areas of study.

Skidmore College
Department of Art and Art History
815 North Broadway
Saratoga Springs, NY 12866-1632
skidmore.edu
Undergraduate degree in studio art in animation, ceramics, communication design, drawing, fiber, metals, painting, photography, printmaking, and sculpture.
Undergraduate major or minor in art history.

Spokane Art School
920 North Howard Street
Spokane, WA 99201
spokaneartschool.org
Offers workshops in ceramics, drawing, glass, jewelry, mixed media, painting, photography, and sculpture.
Adult classes, youth classes, and master classes also offered.

Springfield Museum of Art Classes
107 Cliff Park Road
Springfield, OH 45501
spfld-museum-of-art.org/classes

Classes include illustrating, basic drawing, calligraphy, oil and
watercolor painting, jewelry, stained glass, cartooning, basketry,
pottery, life drawing and sculpting, and art history.
Courses offered for children and adults, beginners and professionals.

Taos Art School
Taos, NM 87571
http://taosartschool.org
Offers classes in painting, weaving, potterymaking, creativity, Native
American arts, basketry, and photography.

Thirdstone Art Works
3997 64th Street
Saugatuck, MI 49423
thirdstoned.com
Courses offered in flameworked glass (beadmaking and small
sculpture), stained-glass design and construction, handmade paper,
jewelry and metalworking, and drawing and painting in many media.

University of Massachusetts—Dartmouth
College of Visual and Performing Arts
284 Old Westport Road
North Dartmouth, MA 02747
umassd.edu/cvpa
Bachelor's degrees in art education, art history, illustration, graphic
design/letterform, photographic/electronic imaging, ceramics,
jewelry/metals, textile design/fiber arts, painting/2-D studies,
sculpture/3-D studies, and music.
Master's degrees: M.F.A. in visual design, artisanry, and fine arts; M.A.E.
in art education.
Certificate programs also offered in fine arts and artisanry.

University of New Hampshire
Department of Art and Art History
Paul Creative Arts Center
30 College Road
Durham, NH 03824
arts.unh.edu

B.A. art (studio art or art history); B.F.A. with emphasis in painting, drawing, sculpture, photography, printmaking, ceramics, and furniture design/woodworking; minors in arts and architectural studies.

M.F.A. in painting.

University of the Arts
320 South Broad Street
Philadelphia, PA 19102
uarts.edu
Offers undergraduate majors in art and design, media and communication, and the performing arts.
Graduate majors in art education/teaching, book arts/printmaking, ceramics, industrial design, museum studies, painting, and sculpture.

Vancouver Academy of Art
Office: 1803-1155 Harwood Street
Vancouver, BC V6E 1S1
artacademy.com
Offers intensive, part-time studies in drawing, painting, sculpture, and glass fusing.

Woodstock School of Art
2470 Route 212
P.O. Box 338
Woodstock, NY 12498
woodstockschoolofart.com
Offers classes and workshops in painting, drawing, sculpture, and printmaking.

Worcester Center for Crafts
25 Sagamore Road
Worcester, MA 01605
worcestercraftcenter.org

Offers introductory, intermediate, and advanced adult classes in ceramics, photography, glass, enameling, metals, jewelry, refinishing, weaving and fiber arts, woodworking and woodturning.

Workshops in clay, glass, metals, photography, textiles, and wood are open to beginners and professionals.

A P P E N D I X

ART MUSEUMS

What follows is a sampling of hundreds of museums and galleries in the United States and Canada. Web addresses are provided. Contact the individual institutions for additional information about employment, internship, or volunteer opportunities.

UNITED STATES

Alabama
Birmingham Museum of Art, Birmingham
artsbma.org

Eastern Shore Art Center, Fairhope
easternshoreartcenter.com

Fayette Art Museum, Fayette
fayetteal.org/sections/community/arts.html#museum

Foley Art Center, Foley
foleyartcenter.com

Gadsden Museum of Art, Gadsden
alabamamuseums.org/g_gma.htm

Huntsville Museum of Art, Huntsville
hsvmuseum.org

Kennedy-Douglas Center for the Arts, Florence
flo-tour.org/kdartcenter.html

Mobile Museum of Art, Mobile
mobilemuseumofart.com

Montgomery Museum of Fine Arts, Montgomery
mmfa.org

Wiregrass Museum of Art, Dothan
wiregrassmuseumofart.org

Alaska
Alaska Native Heritage Center, Anchorage
alaskanative.net

Alaska State Museum, Juneau
museums.state.ak.us

Anchorage Museum of History and Art, Anchorage
anchoragemuseum.org

International Gallery of Contemporary Art, Anchorage
igcaalaska.org

Sheldon Jackson Museum, Sitka
museums.state.ak.us/Sheldon%20Jackson/sjhome.html

Sheldon Museum and Cultural Center, Haines
sheldonmuseum.org

Arizona
Amerind Foundation Museum, Dragoon
amerind.org

ASU Arts Museum, Tempe
asuartmuseum.asu.edu

Center for Creative Photography, Tucson
http://dizzy.library.arizona.edu/branches/ccp/home/home.html

Heard Museum of Native Cultures and Art, Phoenix
heard.org

Mesa Arts Center, Mesa
http://mesaarts.com

Museum of Northern Arizona, Flagstaff
musnaz.org

Phippen Museum of Western Art, Prescott
phippenartmuseum.org

Phoenix Art Museum
phxart.org

Scottsdale Museum of Contemporary Art, Scottsdale
scottsdalearts.org/

Tucson Museum of Art, Tucson
tucsonmuseumofart.org

Arkansas

Arkansas Arts Center, Little Rock
arkarts.com

Delta Cultural Center, Helena
deltaculturalcenter.com

Fort Smith Art Center, Fort Smith
ftsartcenter.com

Gallery Mint Museum, Eureka Springs
gallerymint.com

South Arkansas Arts Center, El Dorado
saac-arts.org

University of Arkansas Fine Arts Center Gallery, Fayetteville
uark.edu/~artinfo/gallery.html

California

Alyce de Roulet Williamson Gallery, Pasadena
artcenter.edu/williamson

Asian Art Museum, San Francisco
asiasociety.org

Bakersfield Museum of Art, Bakersfield
bmoa.org

Bedford Gallery, Walnut Creek
bedfordgallery.org

Berkeley Art Museum, Berkeley
bampfa.berkeley.edu

Bowers Museum of Cultural Art, Santa Ana
bowers.org

California Museum of Photography, Riverside
http://cmp1.ucr.edu

Cantor Arts Center, Palo Alto
http://ccva.stanford.edu//

Casa Romantica Cultural Center and Gardens, San Clemente
casaromantica.org

Crocker Art Museum, Sacramento
crockerartmuseum.org

Fisher Gallery, Los Angeles
usc.edu/org/fishergallery

J. Paul Getty Museum, Los Angeles
getty.edu/museum

Mendocino Arts Center, Mendocino
mendocinoartcenter.org

Norton Simon Museum, Pasadena
nortonsimon.org

Orange County Museum of Art, Newport Beach
ocma.net

Palm Springs Art Museum, Palm Springs
psmuseum.org

Triton Museum of Art, Santa Clara
tritonmuseum.org

UCLA Hammer Museum, Los Angeles
hammer.ucla.edu

Colorado
Art Center of Estes Park, Estes Park
artcenterofestes.com

Aspen Art Museum, Aspen
aspenartmuseum.org

Boulder Museum of Contemporary Art, Boulder
bmoca.org

Carbondale Clay Center, Carbondale
carbondaleclay.org

Center for the Visual Arts, Denver
mscd.edu

Dairy Center for the Arts, Boulder
thedairy.org

Denver Art Museum, Denver
denverartmuseum.org

Longmont Museum and Cultural Center, Longmont
http://ci.longmont.co.us/museum/index.htm

Museo de las Americas, Denver
museo.org

Museum of Outdoor Arts, Englewood
moaonline.org

Sangre de Cristo Center for the Arts, Pueblo
sdc-arts.org

Victoria H. Myhren Gallery, Denver
du.edu/art/galleries/myhren/

Connecticut

Aldrich Museum of Contemporary Art, Brookfield
aldrichart.org

Bruce Museum of Art and Science, Greenwich
brucemuseum.org

Center for Contemporary Printmaking, Norwalk
contemprints.org

Davidson Art Gallery, Middletown
wesleyan.edu/dac/home.html

Florence Griswold Museum, Old Lyme
flogris.org

Joseloff Art Gallery, Hartford
hartfordartschool.org/opp_jose.html

Lyman Allan Art Museum, New London
lymanallyn.org

Silvermine Guild Arts Center, New Canaan
silvermineart.org

Stamford Museum and Nature Center, Stamford
stamfordmuseum.org

Wadsworth Atheneum, Hartford
wadsworthatheneum.org

Westport Arts Center, Westport
westportartscenter.org

Delaware

Biggs Museum of American Art, Dover
biggsmuseum.org

Center for the Creative Arts, Yorklyn
ccarts.org

Christina Cultural Arts Center, Wilmington
ccac-de.org

Delaware Art Museum, Wilmington
delart.org

Delaware Center for the Contemporary Arts, Wilmington
thedcca.org

Hardcastle Gallery, Wilnington
hardcastlegallery.com

University Museums, Newark
museums.udel.edu

Winterthur Museum and Country Estate, Winterthur
winterthur.org

District of Columbia

Corcoran Gallery of Art
corcoran.org

District of Columbia Arts Center
dcartscenter.org

Freer Gallery of Art and Arthur M. Sackler Gallery
asia.si.edu

Hirshhorn Museum and Sculpture Garden
http://hirshhorn.si.edu

National Gallery of Art
nga.gov/

National Museum of African Art
nmafa.si.edu/index2.html

National Museum of the American Indian
nmai.si.edu

National Museum of Women in the Arts
nmwa.org

National Portrait Gallery
npg.si.edu

Textile Museum
textilemuseum.org

Transformer Gallery
transformergallery.org

Florida

Bass Museum of Art, Miami
bassmuseum.org

Boca Raton Museum of Art, Boca Raton
bocamuseum.org

Brevard Museum of Art and Science, Melbourne
artandscience.org

Cornell Fine Arts Museum, Winter Park
rollins.edu/cfam/

Cummer Museum of Art and Gardens, Jacksonville
cummer.org

Hibel Museum of Art, Jupiter
hibelmuseum.org

Lighthouse Center for the Arts, Tequesta
lighthousearts.org

Mennello Museum of American Art, Orlando
mennellomuseum.org

Morikami Museum and Japanese Gardens, Delray Beach
morikami.org

Mount Dora Center for the Arts, Mount Dora
mountdoracenterforthearts.org

Museum of Fine Arts, St. Petersburg
fine-arts.org

Philharmonic Center for the Arts, Naples
thephil.org/index2.html

Salvador Dali Museum, St. Petersburg
salvadordalimuseum.org

Visual Arts Center of Northwest Florida, Panama City
vac.org.cn

Georgia

Albany Museum of Art, Albany
albanymuseum.com

Atlanta International Museum, Atlanta
atlantainternationalmuseum.org

Callanwolde Fine Arts Center, Atlanta
callanwolde.org

Dalton Gallery, Decatur
http://daltongallery.agnesscott.edu

Georgia Piedmont Arts Center, Winder
georgiapiedmontartscenter.com

Gertrude Herbert Institute of Art, Augusta
ghia.org

Madison Museum of Fine Art, Madison
madisonmuseum.org

Morris Museum of Art, Augusta
http://themorris.org/

Museum of Arts and Sciences, Macon
masmacon.com

Museum of Design, Atlanta
museumofdesign.org

Spruill Center for the Arts, Atlanta
spruillarts.org

Telfair Museum of Art, Savannah
telfair.org

Hawaii
Bishop Museum, Honolulu
bishopmuseum.org

The Contemporary Museum, Honolulu
tcmhi.org

Gallery Iolani at Windward Community College, Kaneohe
hawaii.edu/artgallery/crossings/wcc.htm

Hana Cultural Center and Museum, Hana
http://hookele.com/hccm/

Honolulu Academy of Arts, Honolulu
honoluluacademy.org

Hui No'eua Visual Arts Center, Maui
huinoeau.com

Kaua'i Museum, Lihu'e
kauaimuseum.org

Maui Arts and Cultural Center, Kahului
mauiarts.org

Ramsay Museum, Honolulu
ramsaymuseum.org

University of Hawaii Art Gallery, Manoa
hawaii.edu/artgallery

Idaho
Boise Art Museum, Boise
boiseartmuseum.org

Center for Arts and History, Lewiston
artsandhistory.org

Eagle Rock Art Museum, Idaho Falls
eaglerockartmuseum.org

Idaho Historical Museum, Boise
idahohistory.net/museum.html

Idaho State University Minds Eye Gallery, Pocatello
isu.edu/stunion/gallery/index.shtml

Prichard Art Gallery, Moscow
uidaho.edu/galleries

Sun Valley Center for the Arts, Sun Valley
sunvalleycenter.org

Illinois
Art Institute of Chicago, Chicago
artic.edu

Arts Center of Highland Park, Highland Park
theartcenterhp.org

Brickton Art Center, Pine Ridge
bricktonartcenter.org/

David and Alfred Smart Museum of Art, Chicago
http://smartmuseum.uchicago.edu

Elmhurst Art Museum, Elmhurst
elmhurstartmuseum.org

Fine Line Creative Arts Center, St. Charles
finelineca.org

Illinois State Museum, Springfield
museum.state.il.us

Krannert Art Museum and Kinkead Pavilion, Champaign
art.uiuc.edu/galleries/kam

Mexican Fine Arts Center Museum, Chicago
mfacmchicago.org

Oriental Institute Museum, Chicago
http://oi.uchicago.edu/OI/MUS/OI_Museum.html

Peace Museum, Chicago
peacemuseum.org

Rockford Art Museum, Rockford
rockfordartmuseum.org

Indiana

Anderson Fine Arts Center, Anderson
andersonart.org

Art Museum of Greater Lafayette, Lafayette
glmart.org

Ball State University Museum of Art, Muncie
bsu.edu/artmuseum/

Chesterton Art Center, Chesterton
chestertonart.com

Evansville Museum of Arts and Science, Evansville
emuseum.org

Indiana State Museum, Indianapolis
state.in.us/ism

Lubeznik Center for the Arts, Michigan City
lubeznikcenter.org

Purdue University Galleries, West Lafayette
cla.purdue.edu/galleries

Richmond Art Museum, Richmond
richmondartmuseum.org

Snite Museum of Art, Notre Dame
nd.edu/~sniteart/

SoFA Gallery, Bloomington
indiana.edu/~sofa/2005

Swope Art Museum, Terre Haute
swope.org/index1.htm

Iowa
Cedar Rapids Museum of Art, Cedar Rapids
crma.org

Des Moines Art Center, Des Moines
desmoinesartcenter.org

Figge Art Museum, Davenport
figgeartmuseum.org

Hearst Center for the Arts, Cedar Falls
hearstartscenter.com

Muscatine Art Center, Muscatine
muscatineartcenter.org

Octagon Center for the Arts, Ames
octagonarts.org

Sioux City Art Center, Sioux City
siouxcityartcenter.org

University of Iowa Museum of Art, Iowa City
uiowa.edu/uima/

Waterloo Center for the Arts, Waterloo
wplwloo.lib.ia.us/arts/

Kansas

Baker Arts Center, Liberal
cityofliberal.com/thingstodo/attractions/bakerarts.html

Beach Museum of Art, Manhattan
k-state.edu/bma/

Coutts Memorial Museum of Art, El Dorado
http://skyways.lib.ks.us/kansas/museums/coutts/index.html

Denton Art Center, Arkansas City
dentonartcenter.com

Hansen Museum, Logan
hansenmuseum.org

Hutchinson Art Center, Hutchinson
hutchinsonartcenter.com

Kauffman Museum, North Newton
bethelks.edu/kauffman/index.html

Mulvane Art Museum of Washburn University, Topeka
washburn.edu/reference/Mulvane

Salina Art Center, Salina
salinaartcenter.org

Spencer Museum of Art, Lawrence
spencerart.ku.edu

Ulrich Museum of Arts, Wichita
http://webs.wichita.edu/?u=ulrich

Wichita Art Museum, Wichita
wichitaartmuseum.org

Kentucky

Fine Arts Center, Henderson
henderson.kctcs.edu/arts

Gateway Regional Center for the Arts, Mt. Sterling
gatewayartscenter.com

Headley Whitney Museum, Lexington
headley-whitney.org

Janice Mason Art Museum, Cadiz
jmam.org

Kentucky Artisan Center, Berea
kentuckyartisancenter.ky.gov

Kentucky Museum of Art Craft, Louisville
kentuckycrafts.org

Portland Museum, Portland
goportland.org

TriArt Gallery, Louisville
http://members.aye.net/~kacf/triart.htm

University of Kentucky Art Museum, Lexington
uky.edu/ArtMuseum/

Louisiana

Alexandria Museum of Art, Alexandria
themuseum.org

Arna Bontemps African American Museum, Alexandria
arnabontempsmuseum.com

Contemporary Arts Center, New Orleans
cacno.org

Louisiana Art and Science Museum, Baton Rouge
lasm.org

LWU Museum of Art, Baton Rouge
lsumoa.com

Newcomb Art Gallery, New Orleans
newcomb.tulane.edu/artindex.html

New Orleans Museum of Art, New Orleans
noma.org

R.W. Norton Art Foundation, Baton Rouge
rwnaf.org

St. Tammany Art Association, Covington
sttammanyart.org

University Art Museum, Lafayette
thehilliard.org

Maine
Bates College Museum of Art, Lewiston
http://abacus.bates.edu/acad/museum/

Bowdoin College Museum of Art, Brunswick
http://academic.bowdoin.edu/artmuseum/

Center for Maine Contemporary Art, Rockport
artsmaine.org

Colby Museum of Art, Waterville
colby.edu/museum/

Davistown Museum, Liberty
davistownmuseum.org

Farnsworth Art Museum and Wyeth Center,
    Rockland
farnsworthmuseum.org

Fine Arts Work Center, Provincetown
fawc.org

Ogunquit Museum of American Art, Ogunquit
ogunquitmuseum.org/

Portland Museum of Art, Portland
portlandmuseum.org

University of Maine Museum of Art, Orono
umma.umaine.edu

Maryland

Academy Art Museum, Easton
art-academy.org

American Visionary Art Museum, Baltimore
avam.org

Baltimore Museum of Art, Baltimore
http://artbma.org/home.html

Contemporary Museum, Baltimore
contemporary.org

Howard County Center for the Arts, Ellicott City
hocoarts.org/center.htm

Mattawoman Creek Art Center, Marbury
mattawomanart.org

Walters Art Museum, Baltimore
thewalters.org

Washington County Museum of Fine Art, Hagerstown
washcomuseum.org

Massachusetts

Addison Gallery of American Art, Andover
andover.edu/addison/home.htm

Art Complex Museum, Duxbury
artcomplex.org

Berkshire Museum, Pittsfield
berkshiremuseum.org

Boston Museum of Fine Arts, Boston
mfa.org

Boston University Art Gallery, Boston
bu.edu/art/

Cahoon Museum of American Art, Cotuit
cahoonmuseum.org

Cape Cod Museum of Art, Dennis
cmfa.org

DeCordova Museum and Sculpture Park, Lincoln
decordova.org

Folk Art Center of New England, Melrose
facone.org

Fuller Craft Museum, Brockton
fullermuseum.org

Griffin Museum of Photography, Winchester
griffinmuseum.org

Massachusetts Museum of Contemporary Art, North Adams
massmoca.org

MIT List Visual Arts Center, Cambridge
http://web.mit.edu/lvac/www/general/index.html

Museum of Bad Art, Boston
museumofbadart.org

Norman Rockwell Museum, Stockbridge
nrm.org

Schoolhouse Galleries, Provincetown
schoolhousecenter.com

Snow Farm—New England Craft Program, Williamsburg
http://216.156.112.18/

Society of Arts and Crafts, Boston
societyofcrafts.org

Whistler House Museum of Art, Lowell
whistlerhouse.org

Michigan

Alfred P. Sloan Museum, Flint
sloanmuseum.com

Cranbrook Art Museum, Bloomfield Hills
cranbrookart.edu/museum

Dennos Museum Center, Traverse City
dennosmuseum.org

Detroit Artists Market, Detroit
detroitartistsmarket.org

Ella Sharp Museum, Jackson
ellasharp.org

Flint Institute of Arts, Flint
flintarts.org

Grand Rapids Art Museum, Grand Rapids
gramonline.org

Kalamazoo Institute of Arts, Kalamazoo
kiarts.org/museum

Lansing Art Gallery, Lansing
lansingartgallery.org

Museum of New Art, Detroit
detroitmona.com

Saginaw Art Museum, Saginaw
saginawartmuseum.org

Urban Institute for Contemporary Art, Grand Rapids
uica.org

Minnesota

College of Visual Arts Gallery, St. Paul
cva.edu/gallery/gallery.htm

Franconia Sculpture Park, Shafer
franconia.org

Frederick R. Weisman Art Museum, Minneapolis
weisman.umn.edu

Goldstein Museum of Design, St. Paul
http://goldstein.che.umn.edu/

Highpoint Center for Printmaking, Minneapolis
highpointprintmaking.org/main

Juxtaposition Arts, Minneapolis
juxtaposition.org

Minneapolis Institute of Art, Minneapolis
artsmia.org

Minneapolis Sculpture Garden, Minneapolis
http://garden.walkerart.org/index.wac

Minnesota Center for Book Arts, Minneapolis
mnbookarts.org

Minnesota Museum of American Art, St. Paul
mmaa.org

Walker Art Center, Minneapolis
walkerart.org

Mississippi
Lauren Rogers Museum of Art, Laurel
lrma.org

Mississippi Museum of Art, Jackson
msmuseumart.org

Ohr O'Keefe Museum of Art, Biloxi
georgeohr.org

Walter Anderson Museum of Art, Ocean Springs
walterandersonmuseum.org

University of Mississippi Museums, Oxford
olemiss.edu/depts/u_museum/index.htm

University of Southern Mississippi Museum of Art,
    Hattiesburg
usm.edu/arts

Missouri
Albrecht Kemper Museum of Art, St. Joseph
albrecht-kemper.org

Contemporary Art Museum, St. Louis
contemporarystl.org

Laumeier Sculpture Park, St. Louis
laumeier.org

Museum of Art and Archaeology, Columbia
http://museum.research.missouri.edu

Museum of Contemporary Religious Art, St. Louis
http://mocra.slu.edu

Pulitzer Foundation for the Arts, St. Louis
pulitzerarts.org

Sheldon Art Galleries, St. Louis
sheldonconcerthall.org/galleries.asp

Woodcock Museum, St. Louis
http://woodcockmuseum.umsl.edu

Montana

Art Museum of Missoula, Missoula
artmissoula.org

C.M. Russell Museum, Great Falls
cmrussell.org

Custer County Art Center, Miles City
ccac.milescity.org

Hockaday Museum of Art, Kalispell
hockadayartmuseum.org

Holter Museum of Art, Helena
holtermuseum.org

Livingston Center for Arts and Culture, Livingston
livingstoncenter.org

Montana Museum of Art and Culture, Missoula
umt.edu/partv/famus

Northcutt Steele Gallery, Billings
msubillings.edu/art/NorthcuttSteeleGallery.htm

Paris Gibson Square Museum of Art, Great Falls
the-square.org

Yellowstone Art Museum, Yellowstone
http://yellowstone.artmuseum.org

Nebraska

Bemis Center for Contemporary Arts, Omaha
bemiscenter.org

Elkhorn Valley Museum, Norfolk
elkhornvalleymuseum.org

Great Plains Art Museum, Lincoln
unl.edu/plains/gallery/gallery.html

International Quilt Study Center, Lincoln
quiltstudy.org

Joslyn Art Museum, Omaha
joslyn.org

Lux Center for the Arts, Lincoln
luxcenter.org

Museum of Nebraska Art, Kearney
http://monet.unk.edu/mona

Norfolk Arts Center, Norfolk
norfolkartscenter.org

Sheldon Memorial Art Galleries, Lincoln
sheldonartgallery.org

University of Nebraska State Museum, Lincoln
museum.unl.edu

Nevada

Bellagio Gallery of Fine Art, Las Vegas
bellagiolasvegas.com

Brewery Arts Center, Carson City
breweryarts.org

Donna Beam Fine Arts Gallery, Las Vegas
unlv.edu/Colleges/Fine_Arts/Facilities/Donna_Beam_Gallery/

Guggenheim Hermitage Museum, Las Vegas
guggenheimlasvegas.org

Las Vegas Art Museum, Las Vegas
lasvegasartmuseum.org

Nevada Museum of Art, Reno
nevadaart.org

Sierra Arts Center, Reno
sierra-arts.org

St. Mary's Art Center, Virginia City
storey.k12.nv.us/community/stmarys-artcenter/

Western Folklife Center, Elko
westernfolklife.org

New Hampshire

AVA Gallery and Art Center, Lebanon
avagallery.org

Currier Museum of Art, Manchester
currier.org

Hood Museum of Art, Hanover
http://hoodmuseum.dartmouth.edu

Hopkins Center for the Arts, Hanover
http://hop.dartmouth.edu/index.html

Karl Drerup Art Gallery, Plymouth
plymouth.edu/psc/gallery/

Mariposa Museum of World Cultures, Peterborough
mariposamuseum.org

Mt. Kearsarge Indian Museum, Warner
indianmuseum.org

Museum of New Hampshire History, Concord
nhhistory.org/museum.html

Sharon Arts Center, Sharon
sharonarts.org

Thorne-Sagendorph Art Gallery, Keene
keene.edu/tsag

UNH Art Gallery, Durham
unh.edu/art-gallery/

New Jersey
Art School and Gallery at Old Church, Demarest
occcartschool.org

Bergen Museum of Art and Science, Hackensack
thebergenmuseum.com

Grounds for Sculpture, Hamilton
groundsforsculpture.org

Jersey City Museum, Jersey City
jerseycitymuseum.org

Montclair Art Museum, Montclair
montclair-art.com

Morris Museum, Morristown
morrismuseum.org

Museum of American Glass, Millville
wheatonvillage.org/museumamericanglass

Newark Museum, Newark
newarkmuseum.org

Noyes Museum of Art, Oceanville
noyesmuseum.org

Peters Valley Craft Center, Layton
pvcrafts.org

Princeton University Art Museum, Princeton
princetonartmuseum.org

Watchung Arts Center, Watchung
watchungarts.org

Zimmerli Art Museum, New Brunswick
zimmerlimuseum.rutgers.edu

New Mexico

Albuquerque Museum of Art and History, Albuquerque
cabq.gov/museum

Art Center at Fuller Lodge, Los Alamos
artfulnm.org

Georgia O'Keefe Museum, Santa Fe
okeeffemuseum.org

Harwood Museum, Taos
http://harwoodmuseum.org/index_f.php

Millicent Rogers Museum, Taos
http://millicentrogers.org

Museum of Indian Arts and Culture, Santa Fe
miaclab.org

Museum of International Folk Art, Santa Fe
moifa.org

Museum of Spanish Colonial Art, Santa Fe
spanishcolonial.org

Roswell Museum and Art Center, Roswell
roswellmuseum.org

Santa Fe Center for Photography, Sante Fe
santafecenterforphotography.org

Site Sante Fe, Sante Fe
sitesantafe.org

Tamarind Institute, Albuquerque
unm.edu/~tamarind/

Taos Art Museum, Taos
taosartmuseum.org

University Art Gallery, Las Cruces
nmsu.edu/~artgal/

New York
The Alternative Museum, New York
alternativemuseum.org

Bronx Museum of the Arts, Bronx
bronxmuseum.org

Brooklyn Museum of Art, Brooklyn
brooklynmuseum.org

Center for Exploratory and Perceptual Art, Buffalo
http://cepagallery.com/

Center for Photography at Woodstock, Woodstock
cpw.org

Cooper-Hewitt National Design Museum, New York
http://ndm.si.edu

Dahesh Museum of Art, New York
daheshmuseum.org

The Frick Collection, New York
frick.org

Grey Art Gallery, New York
nyu.edu/greyart/

Guggenheim Museum, New York
guggenheim.org

Hudson River Museum, Yonkers
hrm.org

Loeb Art Center, Poughkeepsie
http://fllac.vassar.edu

Neustadt Museum of Tiffany Art, Long Island City
neustadtmuseum.org

New Museum of Contemporary Art, New York
newmuseum.org

Schein-Joseph International Museum of Ceramic Art,
    Almond
http://ceramicsmuseum.alfred.edu/

Storm King Art Center, Mountainville
stormking.org

Studio Museum in Harlem, New York
studiomuseum.org/index1.html

Visual Studies Workshop, Rochester
vsw.org

North Carolina

Asheville Art Museum, Asheville
ashevilleart.org

Contemporary Art Museum, Raleigh
camnc.org

Fayetteville Museum of Art, Fayetteville
fayettevillemuseumart.org

Greenhill Center for North Carolina Art, Greensboro
greenhillcenter.org

Guilford College Art Gallery, Greensboro
guilford.edu/original/libraryart/artgallery/Art.html

Hickory Museum of Art, Hickory
hickorymuseumofart.org/home.php

Light Factory, Durham
lightfactory.org

Louise Wells Cameron Art Museum, Wilmington
cameronartmuseum.com

Nasher Museum of Art, Durham
nasher.duke.edu

North Carolina Pottery Center, Seagrove
ncpotterycenter.com

Penland Gallery, Penland
penland.org/gallery/gallery.html

Sawtooth Center for Visual Art, Winston-Salem
sawtooth.org

Van Every/Smith Galleries, Davidson
www2.davidson.edu/academics/acad_depts/art/galleries/
   galleries.html

North Dakota

The Arts Center, Jamestown
jamestownartscenter.org

North Dakota Museum of Art, Grand Forks
ndmoa.com

Northwest Art Center, Minot
minotstateu.edu/nwac

Pembina State Museum, Bismarck
state.nd.us/hist/mus/pembmus.htm

Plains Art Museum, Fargo
plainsart.org

Taube Museum of Art, Minot
taubemuseum.org

Ohio

Akron Art Museum, Akron
akronartmuseum.org

Artspace/Lima, Lima
artspacelima.com

Butler Institute of American Art, Youngstown
butlerart.com

Canton Museum of Art, Canton
neo.rr.com/cma/

Cleveland Museum of Art, Cleveland
clemusart.com

Columbus College of Art and Design, Columbus
ccad.edu

Contemporary Arts Center, Cincinnati
contemporaryartscenter.org

Dayton Art Institute, Dayton
daytonartinstitute.org

Decorative Arts Center of Ohio, Lancaster
decartsohio.org

Fitton Center for Creative Arts, Hamilton
fittoncenter.org

Ohio Ceramic Center, Crooksville
ohiohistory.org/places/ohceram/

Pyramid Hill Sculpture Park and Museum, Hamilton
pyramidhill.org

Reinberger Galleries, Cleveland
cia.edu/galleries/reinberger/

Oklahoma

Donna Nigh Gallery, Edmond
camd.ucok.edu/events/events_donna_nigh_gallery.html

Fred Jones Jr. Museum of Art, Norman
ou.edu/fjjma/

Guthrie Art Center, Guthrie
guthrieartcenter.org

International Photography Hall of Fame and Museum,
    Oklahoma City
iphf.org

Mabee-Gerrer Museum of Art, Shawnee
mgmoa.com

Melton Gallery, Edmond
camd.ucok.edu/events/events_central_museum_art.html

National Cowboy and Western Heritage Museum, Oklahoma City
nationalcowboymuseum.org

Oklahoma City Art Museum, Oklahoma City
okcartmuseum.com

Philbrook Museum of Art, Tulsa
philbrook.org

Untitled Art Space, Oklahoma City
1ne3.com

World Organization of China Painters Museum, Oklahoma City
theshop.net/wocporg/

Oregon

Coos Art Museum, Coos Bay
coosart.org

Corvallis Arts Center, Corvallis
artcentric.org/cac_about.htm

Four Rivers Cultural Center and Museum, Ontario
4rcc.com

Grants Pass Museum of Art, Grants Pass
gpmuseum.com

Photography at Oregon, Eugene
photographyatoregon.org

Portland Institute for Contemporary Art, Portland
pica.org/index_fl.html

Rogue Gallery and Art Center, Medford
roguegallery.org

Springfield Museum, Springfield
springfieldmuseum.com

Wiseman Gallery, Grants Pass
roguecc.edu/galleries/wiseman.asp

Woodburn Art Center, Woodburn
open.org/~wbartctr/

Pennsylvania

Allentown Art Museum, Allentown
allentownartmuseum.org

Barnes Foundation, Merion
barnesfoundation.org

Brandywine River Museum, Chadds Ford
brandywinemuseum.org

Carnegie Museum of Art, Pittsburgh
cmoa.org

Children's Museum of Pittsburgh, Pittsburgh
pittsburghkids.org

Galleries at Moore College of Art, Philadelphia
http://thegalleriesatmoore.org

Philadelphia Museum of Art, Philadelphia
philamuseum.org/main.asp

Pittsburgh Glass Center, Pittsburgh
pittsburghglasscenter.org

The Print Center, Philadelphia
printcenter.org

Susquehanna Art Museum, Harrisburg
sqart.org

Touchstone Center for Craft, Farmington
touchstonecrafts.com

Rhode Island
Bannister Gallery, Providence
www2.ric.edu/banister

Courthouse Center for the Arts, West Kingston
courthousearts.org

David Winton Bell Gallery, Providence
brown.edu/Facilities/David_Winton_Bell_Gallery/

Fine Arts Center, Kingston
uri.edu/artgalleries/

Four Corners Art Center, Tiverton Four Corners
tivertonfourcorners.com/artscenter/

Hunt-Cavanagh Gallery, Providence
providence.edu/art/gallery.html

National Museum of American Illustration, Newport
americanillustration.org/index2.html

Newport Art Museum, Newport
newportartmuseum.com

Rhode Island School of Design Museum of Art, Providence
risd.edu

Warwick Museum of Art, Warwick
warwickmuseum.org

The Wheeler Gallery, Providence
wheelergallery.org

South Carolina

Aiken Center for the Arts, Aiken
aikencenterforthearts.org

Anderson County Arts Center, Anderson
http://andersonartscenter.org

Bob Jones University Museum and Gallery, Greenville
bjumg.org

Center for American Sculpture at Brookgreen Gardens, Pawleys Island
brookgreen.org

Charleston Museum, Charleston
charlestonmuseum.org

Columbia Museum of Art, Columbia
colmusart.org

Fine Arts Center of Kershaw County, Camden
fineartscenter.org

The Franklin G. Burroughs-Simeon B. Chapin Art Museum, Myrtle Beach
myrtlebeachartmuseum.org

Gibbes Museum of Art, Charleston
gibbesmuseum.org

Greenwood Museum, Greenwood
themuseum-greenwood.org

Spartanburg County Museum of Art, Spartanburg
spartanburgartmuseum.org

William Halsey Gallery, Charleston
cofc.edu/halseygallery/homepage.htm

South Dakota

Adams Museum and House, Deadwood
http://adamsmuseumandhouse.org/

Dacotah Prairie Museum, Aberdeen
dacotahprairiemuseum.com

Redlin Art Center, Watertown
redlinart.com

Sioux City Art Center, Sioux Center
siouxcityartcenter.org

South Dakota Art Museum, Brookings
www3.sdstate.edu/Administration/SouthDakota ArtMuseum/

Washington Pavilion of Arts and Science, Sioux Falls
washingtonpavilion.org

Tennessee
Arrowmont School of Arts and Crafts, Gatlinburg
arrowmont.org

Cheekwood Museum of Art, Nashville
cheekwood.org

Dixon Gallery, Memphis
dixon.org

Frist Center for the Visual Arts, Nashville
fristcenter.org/site/default.aspx

Houston Museum of Decorative Arts, Chattanooga
thehoustonmuseum.com

Knoxville Museum of Art, Knoxville
knoxart.org

Leu Art Gallery, Nashville
belmont.edu/art/dept.cfm?idno=125

Manchester Arts Center, Manchester
manchesterartscenter.com

Memphis Brooks Museum of Art, Memphis
brooksmuseum.org

Rose Center and Council for the Arts, Morristown
rosecenter.org

Vanderbilt University Fine Arts Gallery, Nashville
http://sitemason.vanderbilt.edu/gallery

Texas
Amarillo Museum of Art, Amarillo
amarilloart.org

Amon Carter Museum, Fort Worth
cartermuseum.org

Austin Museum of Art, Austin
amoa.org

The Chinati Foundation, Marfa
chinati.org

Contemporary Arts Museum, Houston
camh.org

Creative Arts Center of Dallas, Dallas
creativeartscenter.org

Houston Center for Photography, Houston
hcponline.org

Jack S. Blanton Museum of Art, Austin
blantonmuseum.org

Longview Museum of Fine Art, Longview
lmfa.org

The Menil Collection, Houston
menil.org

Modern Art Museum of Fort Worth, Fort Worth
http://mamfw.org/

Museum of Texas Tech University, Lubbock
depts.ttu.edu/museumttu/

Orange Show Center for Visionary Art, Houston
orangeshow.org

Rice Gallery, Houston
ricegallery.org

Stark Museum of Art, Orange
starkmuseum.org

Utah
Alpine Art Center, Alpine
alpineartcenter.com

Bountiful Davis Art Center, Bountiful
bdac.org

Braithwaite Fine Arts Gallery, Cedar City
suu.edu/pva/artgallery/

Children's Museum of Utah, Salt Lake City
childmuseum.org

Eccles Community Art Center, Ogden
ogden4arts.org

Folk Arts Program, Salt Lake City
folkartsmuseum.org

Kimball Art Center, Park City
kimball-art.org

Shaw Gallery, Ogden
http://departments.weber.edu/dova/

Springville Museum of Art, Springville
shs.nebo.edu/Museum/Museum.html

Utah Museum of Fine Arts, Salt Lake City
umfa.utah.edu

UVSC Woodbury Arts Museum, Orem
uvsc.edu/gallery/

Vermont

Bennington Museum, Bennington
benningtonmuseum.com

Brattleboro Museum and Art Center, Brattleboro
brattleboromuseum.org

Chaffee Center for the Visual Arts, Rutland
vmga.org/rutland/chaffee.html

Fleming Museum, Burlington
uvm.edu/~fleming/

Frog Hollow—Vermont State Craft Center, Middlebury and Manchester
froghollow.org

Grass Roots Arts Center and Community Effort, Hardwick
graceart.org/index2.php

Middlebury College Museum of Art, Middlebury
middlebury.edu/arts/museum/

Shelburne Museum, Shelburne
shelburnemuseum.org

Southern Vermont Arts Center, Manchester
svac.org

Vermont Folklife Center, Middlebury
vermontfolklifecenter.org

Vermont Studio Center, Johnson
vermontstudiocenter.org

Virginia

Art Museum of Western Virginia, Roanoke
artmuseumroanoke.org

Chrysler Museum of Art, Norfolk
chrysler.org

Contemporary Art Center of Virginia, Virginia Beach
cacv.org

Hampton University Museum, Hampton
hamptonu.edu/museum/

Hermitage Foundation Museum, Norfolk
hermitagefoundation.org

Liberty Town Arts Workshop, Fredericksburg
libertytownarts.com

Maier Museum of Art, Lynchburg
http://maiermuseum.rmwc.edu

Muscarelle Museum of Art, Williamsburg
wm.edu/muscarelle/

Sweet Briar College Art Gallery, Sweet Briar
artgallery.sbc.edu/

Torpedo Factory Art Center, Alexandria
torpedofactory.org

Virginia Center for Creative Arts, Amherst
vcca.com

Virginia Museum of Fine Arts, Richmond
vmfa.state.va.us

Washington
Bainbridge Arts and Crafts, Bainbridge Island
bainbridgeartscrafts.org

Bellevue Art Museum, Bellevue
bellevueart.org

Jundt Art Museum, Spokane
gonzaga.edu/Campus+Resources/Museums+and+Libraries/
    Jundt+Art+Museum/default.asp

Maryhill Museum of Art, Goldendale
maryhillmuseum.org

Museum of Glass, Tacoma
museumofglass.org

Museum of Northwest Art, La Connor
museumofnwart.org

Photographic Center Northwest, Seattle
http://pcnw.org/

Seattle Art Museum, Seattle
seattleartmuseum.org

Seward Park Clay Studio, Seattle
sewardparkart.org

Western Bridge, Seattle
westernbridge.org

Western Gallery, Bellingham
http://westerngallery.wwu.edu/

WSU Museum of Art, Pullman
wsu.edu/artmuse/artmuse.html

West Virginia
The Arts Centre, Martinsburg
theartcentre.org

Clay Center for the Arts and Sciences, Charleston
theclaycenter.org

Huntington Museum of Art, Huntington
hmoa.org

South Charleston Museum, South Charleston
geocities.com/scmuseum/

West Virginia Museum of American Glass, Weston
http://members.aol.com/wvmuseumofglass/

West Virginia State Museum and Cultural Center, Charleston
wvculture.org/agency/cultcenter.html

Wisconsin
Charles Allis Art Museum, Milwaukee
cavtmuseums.org/ca/home.html

Chazen Museum of Art, Madison
http://chazen.wisc.edu/

Haggerty Museum of Art, Milwaukee
marquette.edu/haggerty

Latino Arts Inc., Milwaukee
latinoartsinc.org

Leigh Yawkey Woodson Art Museum, Wausau
lywam.org

Madison Museum of Contemporary Art, Madison
mmoca.org

Miller Art Museum, Sturgeon Bay
dcl.lib.wi.us/millerartmuseum.htm

Milwaukee Art Museum, Milwaukee
mam.org

Monroe Arts Center, Monroe
monroeartscenter.com

Rarh-West Art Museum, Manitowoc
rahrwestartmuseum.org

Sharon Lynne Wilson Center for the Arts, Brookfield
wilson-center.com

Sheboygan Art Museum, Sheboygan
art-museum.org/mainmenu.html

Villa Terrace Decorative Arts Museum, Milwaukee
cavtmuseums.org/vt/home.html

Wyoming

Community Fine Arts Center, Rock Springs
cfac4art.com

Laramie Plains Museum, Laramie
laramiemuseum.org

National Museum of Wildlife Art, Jackson Hole
wildlifeart.org

Nelson Museum of the West, Cheyenne
nelsonmuseum.com

University of Wyoming Art Museum, Laramie
uwyo.edu/artmuseum/

Wyoming State Museum, Cheyenne
http://wyomuseum.state.wy.us/

Canada

Appleton Galleries, Vancouver, BC
appletongalleries.com

Arctic Experience Gallery, Hamilton, ON
arcticexperience.com

Art Gallery of Greater Victoria, Victoria, BC
http://aggv.bc.ca

Art Gallery of Newfoundland and Labrador, St. John's, NF
heritage.nf.ca/arts/agnl/default.html

Art Gallery of Ontario, Toronto, ON
ago.net

Awake Studio, Vancouver, BC
awakeart.com

Canadian Museum of Contemporary Photography, Ottawa, ON
http://cmcp.gallery.ca

Canadian Portrait Academy, Vancouver, BC
canadianportraitacademy.com

Coastal Peoples Fine Arts Gallery, Vancouver, BC
coastalpeoples.com

Eastern Edge Gallery, St. John's, NL
easternedge.ca

Edmonton Art Gallery, Edmonton, AB
edmontonartgallery.com

Montreal Museum of Fine Arts, Montreal, Quebec
mbam.qc.ca

National Gallery of Canada, Ottawa, ON
http://national.gallery.ca

Open Space, Victoria, BC
openspace.ca

Power Plant Contemporary Art Gallery, Toronto, ON
harbourfrontcentre.com

Winnipeg Art Gallery, Winnipeg, MB
wag.mb.ca

APPENDIX D

ART BOOKS

This appendix includes a sampling of books on the various aspects of art, listed alphabetically by author. The subjects may cover a particular medium, artist, or period. They are available through any bookseller.

Adams, Ian. *The Art of Garden Photography*. Portland, OR: Timber Press, 2005.

Aharonian, Gregory, and Richard Stim. *Patenting Art and Entertainment: New Strategies for Protecting Creative Ideas*. Berkeley, CA: NOLO, 2004.

Albers, Anni. *Selected Writings on Design*. Lebanon, NH: University Press of New England, 2001.

———. *On Weaving*. Mineola, NY: Dover Publications, 2003.

Arnheim, Rudolf. *The Art of Visual Perception: A Psychology of the Creative Eye, 50th Anniversary Edition*. Berkeley, CA: University of California Press, 2004.

Baird, Cecile. *Painting Light with Colored Pencil*. Cincinnati: North Light Books, 2005.

Barnes, Robert. *Teaching Art to Young Children 4–9*. London: Falmer Press, 2002.

Barnhart, Richard M., ed. *Three Thousand Years of Chinese Painting*. New Haven: Yale University Press, 2002.

Beal, Nancy, and Gloria Bley Miller. *The Art of Teaching Art to Children: In School and at Home*. New York: Farrar Straus and Giroux, 2001.

Beam, Mary Todd. *Celebrate Your Creative Self: Over 25 Exercises to Unleash the Artist Within.* Cincinnati: North Light Books, 2001.

Botero, Fernando. *Botero.* New York: Rizzoli, 2003.

Clark, T.J. *Farewell to an Idea: Episodes from a History of Modernism.* New Haven: Yale University Press, 2001.

Dahl, Caroline A. *Transforming Fabric: Thirty Creative Ways to Paint, Dye, and Pattern Cloth.* Devon, UK: KP Books, 2004.

Davis, Deborah. *Strapless: John Singer Sargent and the Fall of Madame X.* New York: Tarcher, 2003.

De Sartiges, Astrid, and Richard Boutin (photographer). *Handpainting Porcelain.* New York: Watson-Guptill Publications, 2001.

Dewey, John. *Art as Experience.* New York: Perigree Trade, 2005.

Dews, Pat. *Creative Composition and Design.* Cincinnati: North Light Books, 2003.

Doczi, Gyorgy. *The Power of Limits: Proportional Harmonies in Nature, Art, and Architecture.* Boston: Shambhala, 2005.

Doran, Michael, ed. *Conversations with Cezanne (Documents of Twentieth-Century Art).* Berkeley, CA: University of California Press, 2001.

Dorn, Charles M., Stanley S. Madeja, and Frank R. Sabol. *Assessing Expressive Learning: A Practical Guide for Teacher-Directed Authentic Assessment in K–12 Visual Arts Education.* Mahwah, NJ: Lawrence Erlbaum Associates, 2003.

Dorskind, Cheryl Machat. *The Art of Photographing Children.* New York: Amphoto Books, 2004.

Eisner, Elliot W. *The Arts and the Creation of Mind.* New Haven: Yale University Press, 2004.

———, and Michael D. Day, Eds. *Handbook of Research and Policy in Art Education.* Mahwah, NJ: Lawrence Erlbaum Associates, 2004.

Finlay, Victoria. *Color: A Natural History of the Palette.* London: Random House, 2003.

Foster, Hal, ed. *The Anti-Aesthetic: Essays on Postmodern Culture.* New York: New Press, 2002.

———, Rosaline Krauss, Yve-Alain Bois, and Benjamin Buchloh. *Art Since 1900: Modernism, Antimodernism, Postmodernism.* London: Thames and Hudson, 2005.

Foster, Viv. *Anatomy and Figure Drawing Handbook: A Comprehensive Guide to the Art of Drawing the Human Body.* Berkeley, CA: Thunder Bay Press, 2004.

Gardner, Garth. *Careers in Computer Graphics and Animation.* Garth Gardner Co., 2001.

Genette, Gerard, and Dorit Cohn (translator). *Essays in Aesthetics.* Lincoln, NE: University of Nebraska Press, 2005.

Gerdts, William H. *American Impressionism.* 2d ed. New York: Abbeville Press, 2001.

Ghyka, Matila Costiescu. *The Geometry of Art and Life.* Whitefish, MT: Kessinger Publishing, 2004.

Gombrich, Ernst H.J. *Art and Illusion: A Study in the Psychology of Pictorial Representation.* 6th ed. Boston: Phaidon Press, 2004.

Graphic Artists Guild. *Graphic Artists Guild Handbook: Pricing and Ethical Guidelines.* 11th ed. New York: Graphic Artists Guild, 2003.

Grey, Alex. *The Mission of Art.* Boston: Shambhala, 2001.

Hall, Marcia B. *Michelangelo: The Frescoes of the Sistine Chapel.* New York: Harry N. Abrams, 2002.

Harrison, Charles, and Paul Woods, Eds. *Art Theory 1900–2000: An Anthology of Changing Ideas.* 2d ed. Oxford: Blackwell Publishing, 2002.

Hector, Valerie. *The Art of Beadwork: Historic Inspiration, Contemporary Design.* New York: Watson-Guptill Publications, 2005.

Hickey, Lisa. *Design Secrets: Advertising: 50 Real-Life Projects Uncovered.* Gloucester, MA: Rockport Publishers, 2005.

Hirschfeld, John. *Hirschfeld on Line.* New York: Applause Books, 2000.

Hume, Helen D. *A Survival Kit for the Elementary/Middle School Art Teacher.* San Francisco: Jossey-Bass, 2001.

———. *The Art Teacher's Book of Lists.* San Francisco: Jossey-Bass, 2003.

Huyseen, Andreas. *After the Great Divide: Modernism, Mass Culture, Postmodernism (Theories of Representation and Difference).* Ann Arbor, MI: ACLS History E-Book Project, 2001.

Iuppa, Nicholas. *Interactive Design for New Media and the Web.* Woburn, MA: Focal Press, 2001.

Jackman, Ian. *The Artist's Mentor: Inspiration from the World's Most Creative Minds.* New York: Random House Reference, 2004.

Janson, Anthony. *History of Art.* 6th ed. Upper Saddle River, NJ: Prentice-Hall, 2004.

Johnson, Marilyn A. et al. *Louis Comfort Tiffany: Artist for the Ages.* London: Scala Publishers, 2005.

Kandinsky, Wassily. *Concerning the Spiritual in Art.* Indypublish.com, 2005.

Kaplan, Wendy. *The Arts and Crafts Movement in Europe and America: Design for the Modern World 1880–1920.* London: Thames and Hudson, 2004.

Kemp, Linda. *Watercolor Painting Outside the Lines: A Positive Approach to Negative Painting.* Cincinnati: North Light Books, 2004.

Kimmelman, Michael. *The Accidental Masterpiece: On the Art of Life and Vice Versa.* New York: Penguin Press, 2005.

Kocur, Zoya, and Simon Leung, eds. *Theory in Contemporary Art Since 1985.* Oxford: Blackwell Publishers, 2004.

Koda, Harold. *Goddess: The Classical Mode.* New York: Metropolitan Museum of Art, 2003.

Kostelanetz, Richard. *Soho: The Rise and Fall of an Artists' Colony.* Oxford: Routledge, 2003.

Koster, Joan Bouza. *Growing Artists: Teaching Art to Young Children.* 3d ed. Clifton Park, NY: Thomson Delmar Learning, 2004.

Kutch, Kristy Ann. *Drawing and Painting with Colored Pencil: Basic Techniques for Mastering Traditional and Watersoluble Colored Pencils.* New York: Watson-Guptill Publications, 2005.

Leigh, Tera. *The Complete Book of Decorative Painting.* Cincinnati: North Light Books, 2001.

Loebl, Suzanne. *America's Art Museums: A Traveler's Guide to Great Collections Large and Small.* New York: W.W. Norton and Co., 2002.

London, Peter. *Drawing Closer to Nature: Making Art in Dialogue with the Natural World.* Boston: Shambhala, 2003.

Loori, John Daido. *The Zen of Creativity: Cultivating Your Artistic Life.* New York: Ballantine Books, 2004.

Maynard, Patrick. *Drawing Distinctions: The Varieties of Graphic Expression.* Ithaca, NY: Cornell University Press, 2005.

Michels, Caroll. *How to Survive and Prosper as an Artist: Selling Yourself Without Selling Your Soul.* 5th ed. New York: Owl Books, 2001.

Micklewright, Keith. *Drawing: Mastering the Language of Visual Expression.* New York: Harry N. Abrams, 2005.

Mitchell, Mitch. *Visual Effects for Film and Television.* Woburn, MA: Focal Press, 2004.

Newman, Michelle, and Margaret Allyson. *Handpainting Fabric: Easy, Elegant Techniques.* New York: Watson-Guptill Publications, 2003.

Obalil, Deborah, and Caithlin S. Glass, eds. *Artists Communities: A Directory of Residencies that Offer Time and Space for Creativity.* 3d ed. New York: Allworth Press, 2005.

Ormond, Richard, and Elaine Kilmurray. *John Singer Sargent: Portraits of the 1890s.* London: Paul Mellon Center, 2002.

Patterson, Freeman. *Photography and the Art of Seeing.* 3d ed. Toronto: Key Porter Books, 2004.

Perloff, Marjorie. *The Futurist Movement: Avant-Garde, Avant Guerre, and the Language of Rupture.* Chicago: University of Chicago Press, 2003.

Perrella, Lynne. *Artists' Journals and Sketchbooks: Exploring and Creating Personal Pages.* Indianapolis: Quarry Books, 2004.

Perry, Vicky. *Abstract Painting: Concepts and Techniques.* New York: Watson-Guptill Publications, 2005.

Peterson, Brian H., and William H. Gerdts, eds. *Pennsylvania Impressionism.* Philadelphia: University of Pennsylvania Press, 2002.

Peterson's. *Guide to Visual and Performing Arts.* 10th ed. Clifton Park, NY: Peterson's Guides, 2004.

———. *Internships 2005.* 25th ed. Clifton Park, NY: Peterson's Guides, 2004.

Pollock, Gilda. *Mary Cassatt.* Wilkes Barre, PA: Chaucer Press, 2005.

Purcell, Carl. *Painting with Your Artist's Brain: Learn to Paint What You See Not What You Think You See.* Cincinnati: North Light Books, 2004.

Quiller, Stephen. *Color Choices: Making Color Sense Out of Color Theory.* New York: Watson-Guptill Publications, 2002.

Rothko, Mark. *The Artist's Reality: Philosophies of Art.* New Haven: Yale University Press, 2004.

Scott, Jeanne Filler. *Painting Animal Friends.* Cincinnati: North Light Books, 2005.

Spurling, Hilary. *The Unknown Matisse: A Life of Henri Matisse, Volume 1: The Early Years, 1869–1908.* Berkeley, CA: University of California Press, 2001.

Stevens, Mark. *De Kooning: An American Master.* New York: Knopf, 2004.

Stobart, Jane. *Printmaking for Beginners.* New York: Watson-Guptill Publications, 2002.

Stokstad, Marilyn. *Art History Revised.* 2d ed. Upper Saddle River, NJ: Prentice-Hall, 2004.

Tauchid, Rheni. *The New Acrylics: Complete Guide to the New Generation of Acrylic Paints.* New York: Watson-Guptill Publications, 2005.

Vaz, Mark Cotta, and Craig Barron. *The Invisible Art: The Legends of Movie Matte Painting.* San Francisco: Chronicle Books, 2004.

Walker, George A. *The Woodcut Artist's Handbook: Techniques and Tools for Relief Printmaking.* Richmond Hill, ON: Firefly Books, 2005.

Walther, Ingo, and Rainer Metzger. *Van Gogh: The Complete Paintings.* Koln: Taschen, 2002.

Wang, Jianan, and Xiaoli Cai. *Oriental Painting Course: A Structured, Practical Guide to the Painting Skills and Techniques of China and the Far East.* New York: Watson-Guptill Publications, 2001.

Wayne, Kenneth. *Modigliani and the Artists of Montparnasse.* New York: Harry N. Abrams, 2002.

Weintraub, Linda. *In the Making: Creative Options for Contemporary Art.* Zzdap Publishing, 2003.

Whyte, Mary. *An Artist's Way of Seeing.* Charleston, SC: Wyrick and Co., 2005.

Wolf, Rachel Rubin. *The Acrylic Painter's Book of Styles and Techniques.* Cincinnati: North Light Books, 2001.

Zeki, Semir. *Inner Vision: An Exploration of Art and the Brain.* Oxford: Oxford University Press, 2000.

APPENDIX E

ART FAIRS AND EXPOS

The following list is a sampling of art fairs and expos where art lovers can view and purchase art, and where artists can sell their work. Visit the web sites for specific information on dates, times, and locations.

AIPAD
Association of International Photography Art Dealers
New York, NY
Show features 82 international exhibitors displaying vintage and
   contemporary fine art photography.

Around the Coyote Art Festival
Chicago, Illinois
aroundthecoyote.org
Hundreds of painters, photographers, sculptors, actors, performers,
   dancers, poets, and filmmakers participate in this unique opportunity
   to exhibit and sell their work to visitors from all over the United
   States.

Art Chicago in the Park
Chicago, Illinois
artchicago.com
An international contemporary art fair for the display and
   sale of works.

Art Miami

Miami, Florida

art-miami.com

Includes 125 participating galleries from 26 countries. The Currents
section focuses on new talent, while project spaces and a program of
panel discussions designed to provide close-up commentary on a
broad range of topics round out the Art Miami experience.

Broad Ripple Art Fair

Indianapolis, Indiana

indygreenways.org/pedalpark/braf.htm

More than 200 artists show and sell their fine art and fine craft work in a
parklike setting. Other activities include music, a children's area, a
gourmet food court, and the opportunity to explore the year-round
activities of the Indianapolis Art Center.

Brookline Artists' Open Studios

Brookline, Massachusetts

Annual open studios event for participating Brookline artists. Sponsored
by the Brookline Council for Art and Humanities and Massachusetts
Cultural Council.

Carefree Fine Art and Wine Festival

Thunderbird Artists

Fountain Hills, AZ 85268

thunderbirdartists.com/festivals/carefreefineartwinefestival.shtml

Carefree is in the Sonoran Desert, 20 minutes north of Scottsdale. The
streets of Carefree are closed and turned into a festival that includes 165
juried artists, wine and microbrew tastings, and musical entertainment.

Celebration of Fine Art

Scottsdale, Arizona

http://phoenix.about.com/od/attractionsandevents/ss/celebart.htm

Artists from across the country exhibit in a variety of media, including
oil, watercolor, sculpture, photography, jewelry, ceramics, baskets,
furniture, and contemporary mixed media. A sculpture exhibition
with life-size and monumental sculpture is located in the central
courtyard of the show. This is a unique event that combines the

casual and relaxed atmosphere of a street fair with the high-quality art found in an art gallery.

Central Pennsylvania Festival of the Arts
State College, Pennsylvania
arts-festival.com
The festival is a celebration of the visual and performing arts, featuring over 300 artists from the United States and Canada.

Cleveland Christmas Connection
Cleveland, Ohio
christmasconnections.com
Offers more than 900 booths of arts, crafts, retail, and decorating items for sale.

Festival of Arts
Pageant of the Masters
Newport Beach, California
foapom.com/site/pageant.asp
An annual exhibit of original artworks.

FOTOfusion
Delray Beach, Florida
fotofusion.org
Festival includes photography auction, portfolio appraisals by experts, seminars and panel discussions, appraisals, and exhibitions.

Freedom Festival
Blue Ridge Artists and Crafters Association
Lake Junaluska, North Carolina
braca.org
Displays fine art works and hand-crafted items.

Heart of Virginia Festival
Farmville, Virginia
http://heartofvirginia.org/indexA.html
A celebration of the arts, culture, and music of southside Virginia.

Mable House Artfest
Mableton, Georgia
artshow.com/MableHouse/artfestnew.html
An outdoor festival featuring fine arts, country crafts, art and craft
 demonstrations, children's activities, entertainment, and food
 concessions with a focus on the heritage of the community.

Melbourne Art Festival
Melbourne, Florida
melbournearts.org
A two-day festival featuring 250 artists working in graphics, sculpture,
 painting, photography, jewelry, ceramics, and other media.

New York Arts of Pacific Asia Show
New York, NY
caskeylees.com/shows/4/asian/ny/
An antiques fair exhibiting Chinese ceramics, textiles, and jade as well as
 Japanese works of art.

New York Ceramics Fair
New York, NY
caskeylees.com/shows/6/ceramics/ny/
Displays antique and contemporary works in ceramics, enamels, and glass.

Outsider Art Fair
New York, NY
sanfordsmith.com/out.html
Includes art dealers from around the world.

Pacific Northwest Arts Fair
Bellevue, Washington
wmgallery.com/bellevue/default.htm
http://bellevueart.org/craftsfair/index.htm
Features more than 300 U.S. and Canadian artists selected by an
 independent jury.

Palm Beach 3
West Palm Beach, FL 33401
palmbeach3.com

Features three distinct and complementary art fairs in one location. A combination of leading international galleries presents contemporary art, classical and contemporary photography, and decorative arts and contemporary design.

Photo LA
Los Angeles, California
artfairsinc.com/photola/2006/
The largest and longest running photographic art fair in the West.

Renaissance in Rehoboth
210 Savannah Road
Lewes, DE 19958
http://rehobothtoday.com/Renaissance/
A nine-week celebration of art that takes place throughout the entire Delaware coastal region.

San Francisco Fine Print Fair
San Francisco, California
printdealers.com/printfairs.cfm?id=88
Eighteen fine art dealers from the United States and Canada exhibit and sell inventories comprising five centuries of fine prints ranging from the Old Masters to Contemporary. Offers opportunities to view and buy original works by many major and minor artists.

San Francisco International Art Exposition
sfiae.com
Featuring more than 75 international galleries representing more than 2,000 artists, the show is a collection of modern and contemporary artwork in a variety of artistic styles and media that range from painting, drawing, photography, and printmaking, to sculpture, video, installation, and mixed media.

San Francisco Tribal and Textile Arts Show
San Francisco, California
caskeylees.com/shows/8/tribal/sf/
Show features the collections of 80 international dealers-galleries who specialize in museum-quality, pre-1940's tribal, textile, and folk art.

Collectors and the general public alike have a chance to view and purchase cultural artifacts of indigenous peoples from around the world.

Seattle Print Fair
seattleprintfair.com
Eighteen fine art dealers from around the country exhibit original prints and other works on paper. The fair provides an opportunity to meet knowledgeable print experts and discuss original prints from the 15th century to the present. From miniature bookplates by contemporary artists to museum-quality drawings by modern masters, all works displayed at the fair are for sale.

Skokie Art Guild's 38th Annual Art Fair
Lincolnwood, Illinois
skokienet.org/saguild1/artfair.html
A fine art fair with more than 65 exhibitors.

Sonoran Festival of Arts
Cave Creek, Arizona
sonoranartsleague.org/festfacts.html
Festival features local and nationally acclaimed painters, sculptors, jewelers, wood and glass artists, photographers, and artists working with mixed media.

Three Rivers Arts Festival
Pittsburgh, Pennsylvania
artsfestival.net
A visual and performing arts festival that includes a juried visual arts exhibition, an artists' market with more than 400 crafters and artists, daily performances on five stages, and exhibitions of local and national artists in various indoor and outdoor sites throughout downtown Pittsburgh and Point State Park.

Watermedia
Pikes Peak Watercolor Society
Colorado Springs, Colorado
pcisys.net/~ppwsart/

An international juried exhibit and show that's held at a different
location in the Pikes Peak region of Colorado each year.

The Western Design Conference
Cody, Wyoming
http://walkingstar.com/wdc1/html/about.html
Crafts people showcase original work in furniture, fashion, jewelry, and
home accessories. The seminar series is tailored for professionals,
with programming that focuses on specific design topics. The
conference's fashion show allows a sneak peak into the hottest western
couture collections of the year.

ABOUT THE
AUTHOR

A full-time writer of career books, Blythe Camenson's main professional concern is helping job seekers make educated choices. She firmly believes that with enough information, readers can find long-term, satisfying careers. To that end, she researches traditional as well as unusual occupations, talking to a variety of professionals about what their jobs are really like. In all her books, she includes firsthand accounts from people who reveal what to expect in each occupation, the upsides as well as the down.

Camenson's interests range from history and photography to writing novels. She is also director of Fiction Writer's Connection, a membership organization providing support to new and published writers, and maintains a web site at www.fictionwriters.com.

Camenson was educated in Boston, earning her B.A. in English and psychology from the University of Massachusetts, and her M.Ed. in counseling from Northeastern University.

In addition to *Careers in Art*, Blythe Camenson has written various other career books for McGraw-Hill.